FOR REFERENCE

Do Not Take From This Room

NOV 6 '92

The Gulf War

The
MILITARY HISTORY
of the
UNITED STATES

Christopher Chant

The Gulf War

MARSHALL CAVENDISH
NEW YORK · LONDON · TORONTO · SYDNEY

NOV 6 '92

Library Edition Published 1992

(C) Marshall Cavendish Limited 1992

Published by
Marshall Cavendish Corporation
2415 Jerusalem Avenue
PO Box 587
North Bellmore
New York 11710

Series created by Graham Beehag Book Design

The publishers wish to thank the following organizations
who have supplied photographs:

The National Archives, Washington. United States
Navy, United States Marines, United States Army,
United States Air Force, Department of Defense,
Library of Congress, The Smithsonian Institution.

The publishers gratefully thank David Paradine Television Inc. for allowing the use of parts of an interview
from the television broadxcast *General H. Norman
Schwarzkopf Talking With David Frost.*

Series Editor	Maggi McCormick
Consultant Editors	James R. Arnold
	Roberta Wiener
Sub Editor	Julie Cairns
Designer	Graham Beehag
Illustrators	John Batchelor
	Steve Lucas
	Terry Forest
	Colette Brownrigg
Indexer	Mark Dartford

Library of Congress Cataloging-in-Publication Data

Chant, Christopher.
  The Military History of the United States / Christopher Chant –
Library ed.
    p. cm.
  Includes bibliographical references and index.
  Summary: Surveys the wars that have directly influenced the
United States., from the Revolutionary War through the Cold War.
  ISBN 1-85435-366-7 ISBN 1-85435-361-9 (set)
  1. United States - History, Military - Juvenile literature.
 |1. United States - History, Military.| 1. Title.
t181.C52 1991
973 - dc20   90 - 19547
                                                    CIP
                                                    AC

Printed in Singapore by Times Offset PTE Ltd
Bound in the United States

Contents

The end of the Vietnam War marked a major turning point in American military history. The Korean War had demonstrated the reluctance of the American people to support a long "no win" war, and this reluctance was more than confirmed by the increasingly hostile response of the public to the Vietnam War. The two wars therefore served to reinforce the traditional suspicions of the military establishment and military adventurism. They also strengthened public disagreement – and anger – in the cases where the administration sought to use military-strength diplomacy as the primary instrument of American policy.

Public distrust of the military establishment can take either (or indeed both) of two apparently conflicting forms. In a limited conflict that becomes unpopular, the public tends to accuse the military establishment of bloodthirstiness for fighting the war in the first place. If the conflict starts to lengthen, the public condemns the establishment for faint-heartedness if it tries to avoid fighting in the "American military way," with all the massive strength and capability available to it.

These two views are simplifications of the types of accusation leveled at the military during the Vietnam War by the adherents of left- and right-wing political philosophies respectively. Even after the pullout from Vietnam, the military maintained a strength of two million or more people, which helped to raise a small but nonetheless potent fear of the influence that the military might exercise over the government, and the more remote concern that a coup could be launched by the military. This last possibility has always been a specter rather than a fear with any real substance.

A Military-Industrial Complex?

The size of the military establishment combined with the large segment of the

The Lockheed F-117A "Stealth" warplane was used only in modest numbers during the war with Iraq, but it played a part out of all proportion with its numbers. It could avoid detection to deliver its small load of precision-guided weapons with devastating accuracy.

The angular, faceted contours of the F-117A are designed to reflect the energy of an enemy's radar in any direction except back toward the transmitter/receiver unit, which removes the chance of producing a radar ''echo.'' Another way in which detectivity is reduced is to mix the engines' hot exhaust gases with cold, freestream air to reduce the chance of infrared (heat) detection. This is an F-117A of the 37th Tactical Fighter Wing in a Saudi Arabian hangar.

economy wholly or largely dependent on it introduces another fear: the existence of a military-industrial complex so strong and pervasive that it can affect some aspects of national policy directly. There is also a feeling that the strength of the American military machine might convince some administrations that they could forgo a diplomatic solution to some international crises in favor of a military option. The lessons of the Korean and Vietnam Wars prove that a little credence should be given to this thought.

The overall suspicion of the military establishment and its position in American life was responsible, at least in part, for the 1974 decision that U.S. forces should revert to their traditional, all-volunteer basis.

Diplomatic and associated military factors were still looming large in the minds of the American public during the 1980 presidential and congressional elections. These elections turned quite conclusively on matters of foreign policy and national security, resulting in victories for

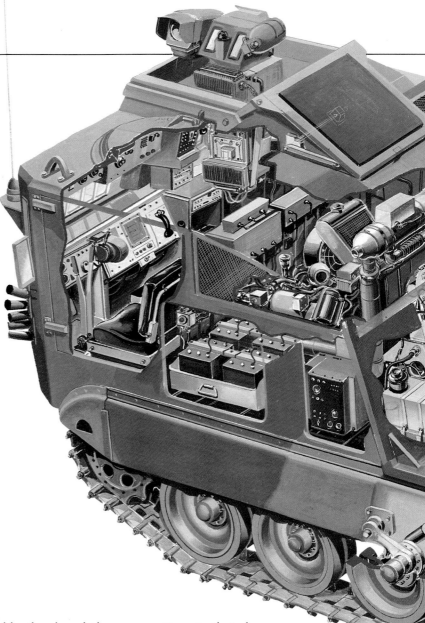

the Republicans in both elections. Ronald Reagan won the presidential election by a landslide 489 electoral college votes to incumbent President Carter's 49. More indicative of the American mood, however, was the 55-to-46 Republican majority in the Senate. It was only the third time since 1930 that the Republicans had had a Senate majority.

Public Opinion Shifts to the Right

It was thus perfectly clear that the American people wanted a change in national security policy, and a single episode highlighted this need most clearly. The sense of public humiliation felt at President Carter's handling of the Tehran hostage crisis was heightened by the bungled rescue attempt that he eventually authorized. Closely following these twin humiliations was the Senate's refusal to ratify the second Strategic Arms Limitation Talks treaty with the U.S.S.R. in tacit admission that the Soviets were now ahead of the Americans not only in conventional military forces, but also in nuclear capability.

The Reagan administration took office in January 1981 faced with the need to reassess completely national security requirements and the forces needed to fulfill these requirements. The most important element in this complex equation was the nature of U.S.-Soviet relations. In historical terms, the nature of the Soviet threat and the American response to it dated from March 1947 and the announcement of the "Truman Doctrine."

Ronald Reagan
For further references see pages
13, 14, 16, 19, 20, 27, 52

Jimmy Carter
For further references see pages
14, 16, 18, *19*, 20, 25

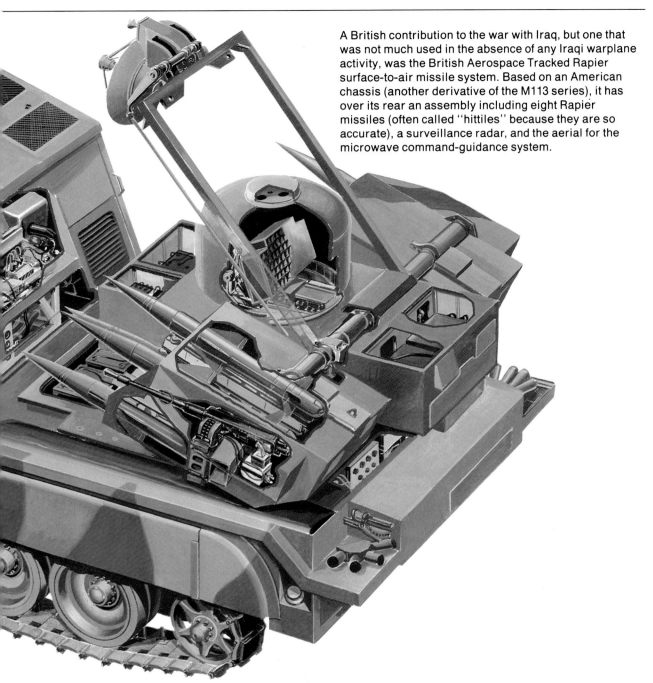

A British contribution to the war with Iraq, but one that was not much used in the absence of any Iraqi warplane activity, was the British Aerospace Tracked Rapier surface-to-air missile system. Based on an American chassis (another derivative of the M113 series), it has over its rear an assembly including eight Rapier missiles (often called "hittiles" because they are so accurate), a surveillance radar, and the aerial for the microwave command-guidance system.

This was based on the belief that the U.S.S.R. was determined to expand certainly into Europe, probably into the Middle East, and possibly into Asia. This overall assessment of Soviet ambitions led to the policy known as the Truman Doctrine, designed to contain Soviet expansion wherever and whenever it might be found. The doctrine was one of the spurs to the creation of the North Atlantic Treaty Organization, together with a large and permanent American military presence in Europe.

Revised Perceptions of the Soviet Threat

As early as 1948, however, some political and academic figures in the U.S. began to doubt that the Soviets were determined to expand. They suggested instead that Soviet moves around the world were designed to check the encirclement of Soviet interests by the United States and its allies. This revisionist assessment of Soviet policies was generally ridiculed at

The most important fighter plane used in the fleet-defense role by U.S. Naval Aviation in the Middle East was the Grumman F-14A Tomcat. This machine of the U.S.S. *Independence*'s air wing has a decidedly "used" appearance. It is preparing to take on fuel from a Boeing KC-135 Stratotanker of the U.S. Air Force's 70th Air Refueling Squadron over the Persian Gulf. The Tomcat carries four air-to-air missiles on its glove hardpoints, namely two AIM-7 Sparrow medium-range and two AIM-9 Sidewinder short-range weapons.

the time. The most telling point against the revisionist's assessment was that between 1939 and 1945, the U.S.S.R. had seized 180,000 square miles of territory (all three of the Baltic states as well as parts of Finland, Poland, and Romania) and after World War II had annexed from Japan the southern part of Sakhalin Island and four of the Kurile Islands. As the 1940s and 1950s continued, the U.S.S.R. acquired a still larger "empire" of European satellites and the bastion of North Korea. Over the same period, it was pointed out, the U.S.A. had granted independence to the Philippines, and the nation's European allies were slowly but steadily moving toward independence for their African and Asian colonies. Given these circumstances, the revisionist assessment managed to gain only modest credibility, notably in academic circles, during the 1950s and early 1960s, but it never secured a decisive breakthrough.

As American superiority in strategic nuclear weapons was eroded by the huge

Soviet efforts of the 1950s and 1960s, another academic and diplomatic idea appeared. This suggested that the two superpowers were arriving at a position of strategic equality (or parity) with each other. Each superpower was therefore vulnerable to the other's strategic nuclear arsenal and equally invulnerable to every other form of military strength. In this circumstance, the new school of thought suggested, the only sensible course of action was *detente:* the two superpowers would learn to live with each other, and as less antagonistic policies were adopted, an era of world peace would begin.

A Policy of Detente

This policy of detente, or easier relations with the U.S.S.R., gained limited backing in the time of Presidents John F. Kennedy and Lyndon B. Johnson (1961-1969), but it was not until the administration of

President Richard M. Nixon (1969-1974) that detente was adopted as official policy, chiefly through the efforts of Secretary of State Henry Kissinger. According to Nixon and Kissinger, the American and Soviet nuclear arsenals had become so large and powerful that the concept of a winnable war between the superpowers was no longer in the realm of reality. In this situation, the administration argued, the time was ripe for a more stable and less crisis-ridden relationship between the U.S.A. and the U.S.S.R., with national security provided by invulnerable second-strike forces (nuclear weapons that would survive any first attack by the other side and thus be able to inflict massive retaliation).

The policy of detente went a considerable way to reducing the possibility of nuclear war between the superpowers. There remained the dangers of limited war and local conflict, and either could escalate into larger and more dangerous confrontations between the superpowers. The policy of detente opened the way for agreements that "replaced confrontation with negotiation." Both Nixon and Kissinger claimed that this tendency was evident in the first Strategic Arms Limitation Talk agreements in May 1972 and June 1973, which brought about a new and considerably less tense era in U.S. relations with the Soviets.

The Death of Detente

However, it became clear as early as 1973, the golden age of detente, that the Soviets were supplying increasingly sophisticated weapons to their client states in the "third world." In October 1973, for example, operations in the "Yom Kippur War" between Israel and her Arab neighbors saw the extensive use by Egypt and Syria of such Soviet weapons as advanced antitank and surface-to-air missile systems. Over the next five years,

Still one of the most important attack warplanes operated by the U.S. Navy, the Vought A-7 Corsair II is subsonic, but can carry a heavy warload. This A-7E of the VA-72 squadron embarked on the carrier U.S.S. *John F. Kennedy*, is seen here on a mission over Iraq, with one AIM-9 Sidewinder for self-protection and triplets of "Rockeye" cluster bombs under the wings for attacks on Iraqi armored formations.

the U.S.S.R. continued to export large quantities of conventional weapons, and by 1978, it had overtaken the U.S. as the world's largest exporter of weapons. Negotiations about ways to limit the transfer of conventional weapons proved fruitless. This confirmed what had already been suggested – that it was impossible to divide superpower confrontation into separate compartments. An eased direct confrontation at the nuclear level heightened the possibility of an indirect confrontation at the conventional level, with the latter revolving largely around the involvement of the superpowers in third-party conflicts. And it became clear as early as October 1973, when the U.S.S.R. alerted its airborne intervention force and the U.S.A. brought its strategic nuclear forces to a higher level of preparation during the crisis of the "Yom Kippur War," that third-party conflicts could still cause an escalation of superpower confrontation.

Superpower detente was soon put under severe strain. The Soviets began to deploy the first examples of their new SS-18 "Satan," a fourth-generation intercontinental ballistic missile, which increased the nuclear threat to the U.S.A. and destabilized the balance between the superpowers. The Department of Defense warned that, by the 1980s, the U.S.S.R. would need to use only a small part of its first-strike capability to destroy between 80 and 90 percent of the LGM-30 Minuteman force that was the mainstay of the land-based American nuclear deterrent. This threat would destabilize the superpower balance even more and would leave the U.S. with the choice of negotiating under unfavorable conditions, or relying on the UGM-73 Poseidon submarine-launched ballistic missile. Less accurate than the Minuteman, the Poseidon was intended to destroy cities rather than to "surgically" eliminate Soviet missile sites.

The M1 Abrams was designed as successor to the M60 series of main battle tanks and was planned with the European theater as its anticipated operating region. The type was developed by General Dynamics to meet a requirement that demanded significant improvements over the M60 in armament, protection, mobility, reliability, availability, maintainability, and durability. It was planned for a 120-mm (4.72-inch) caliber M256 smoothbore gun firing fin-stabilized ammunition, to be installed eventually, but pending availability of this weapon, the initial M1 Abrams model that entered service in 1980 was fitted with the standard 105-mm (4.13-inch) caliber M68 rifled gun, an American development of the British L7 series weapon. The M1A1 model that entered service in 1986 is the first variant fitted with the M256, an American development of the German Rh-120 series weapon.

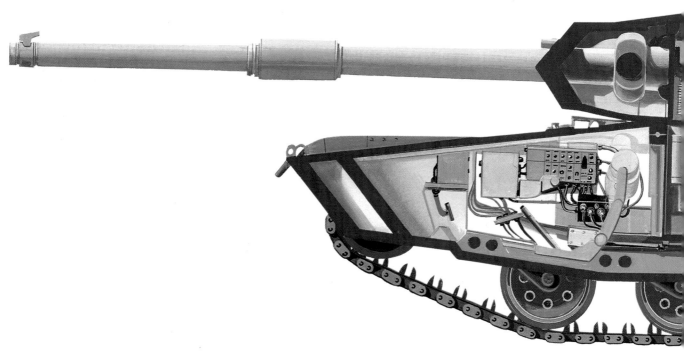

By the late 1970s, the policy of detente was clearly obsolete, and President Gerald R. Ford forbade the use of the word during his administration (1974-1977). Detente was effectively killed by the Soviet invasion of Afghanistan in December 1979, whereupon the Senate rejected the SALT II treaty.

Reagan and a Stronger United States

Ronald Reagan campaigned on a platform that included a more forceful foreign policy backed by improved military strength. Negotiations between the superpowers continued, and each side agreed to abide by the terms of the unratified SALT II treaty as the Strategic Arms Reduction Talks got underway. Reagan's more dynamic approach to foreign policy and his buildup of U.S. military strength slowly began to yield

dividends, and the stubbornness of the Soviets under Leonid Brezhnev began to break down. This process was accelerated by Brezhnev's death and replacement by Yuri Andropov, who soon died and was replaced by Mikhail Gorbachev.

Throughout the Reagan administration, the main preoccupation of the U.S. forces remained the situation in Europe, which typically absorbed 217,000 troops from a 1986 total of 780,650 personnel. The other main area of concern was Asia. When the Nixon administration began in 1969, the Asian commitment, particularly the Vietnam War, absorbed larger numbers of troops than Europe, reaching its peak at 550,000. In 1969, U.S. service commitments were sized and structured for a "two-and-one-half war" capability; policy demanded that the U.S should be able to fight a NATO war against the Warsaw Pact in Europe, a war against Communist China in Asia, and a limited war elsewhere on the globe simultaneously.

Mikhail Gorbachev
For further references see pages
22, 77, 79, 121

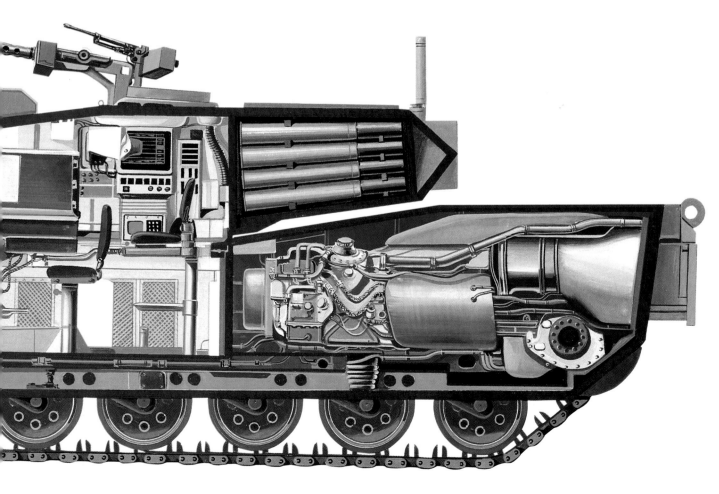

This massive U.S. commitment was scaled down, but it resulted not in strength reductions, but in a gradual withdrawal of American forces from Vietnam to the continental U.S.A.. Between 1969 and 1975, 702,000 American personnel were pulled back from Southeast Asia, but not a single person from Europe. The American concentration on Europe was thus emphasized, and the administration's policy changed to one of troops for Europe and money for Asia. The rationale for this alteration was the administration's belief that the Chinese threat to the noncommunist nations of Asia and to U.S. national security interests was significantly less than it had been during the 1960s. Kissinger made a secret visit to China in 1971, which paved the way for a highly successful visit by President Nixon in 1972. Full diplomatic relations between the U.S. and China were not restored at this time, but by the end of the Ford administration, Nixon's aim that "Asian hands must shape the Asian future" had begun to happen.

U.S. Relations with the Far East

Even so, it was clear at the beginning of the Carter administration to political and military planners alike that Japan and South Korea continued to play an important part in overall U.S. global strategy. Allied to this was the belief that it would benefit U.S. interests to capitalize on the continued friction between the U.S.S.R. and China. While the U.S. was no longer prepared to play a major role in Southeast Asian affairs, it considered events in Northeast Asia to be vital to American strategic considerations. Even so, the Carter administration found it difficult to turn this concept into effective policies.

After the Korean War in 1953, relations between South Korea and the U.S. had gone up and down, but in general become worse. In 1971, for example, Nixon decided that the 7th Infantry Division should be pulled out of South Korea. In December of the same year, President Park ordered a state of emergency in South Korea, followed by a state of martial law in October 1972. In December of that year, a new constitution gave Park virtually dictatorial powers. Park soon issued four emergency decrees and ordered the arrest of several leading opponents, including a former president. Park and his supporters said that the moves were essential because of the worsening situation in the area, while his opponents claimed that Park was exploiting the U.S. withdrawal to extend his power at a time when his popular support was declining steadily.

The feelings of the South Korean opposition were mirrored in Washington. There was talk of relocating or even removing the other U.S. formation in South Korea, the 2nd Infantry Division, which was deployed along the demilitarized zone on the only logical approach route to Seoul from North Korea. Such talk was probably designed to warn Park's government against too high-handed an approach to the opposition, and in fact it ended after the collapse of South Vietnam in April 1975. In the following month, President Ford confirmed that there would be no alteration in the American commitment to South Korea, and in August of the same year Secretary of Defense James A. Schlesinger visited Seoul to confirm that U.S. forces would remain in South Korea and that American aid would still be provided for the upgrading of South Korea's forces.

In the 1976 presidential elections, Carter called for the removal of U.S. forces and tactical nuclear weapons from South Korea. Only one week after Carter's inauguration, Vice President Walter Mondale announced that American forces in South Korea would be withdrawn, but only after consultations with the South Korean and Japanese governments. In the face of bitter opposition from the South Korean government, the withdrawal started very slowly, but in 1979 it was halted (supposedly until 1982) when three of the 2nd Infantry Division's brigades were still in place. The withdrawal was cancelled after the inauguration of President Reagan in January 1981, leaving the U.S. Army with some 29,750 men in South Korea to the present day.

Since the postponement and then cancellation of the plan to remove the 2nd Infantry Division, U.S. relations with South Korea have continued their seesaw course, but the general trend has been upward despite hiccups such as the violent

Marine U.S., Marine Corps, Saudi Arabia, 1991

This marine is seen in typical combat dress for Operation "Desert Storm." The core of his outfit is the Desert BDU (Battledress Uniform) worn with the olive drab ALICE (All-purpose Lightweight Individual Combat Equipment) nylon support webbing and the Kevlar "Fritz" helmet of the PASGT (Personal Armor System, Ground Troops) system with camouflaged cover. Protection against nuclear, biological, and chemical warfare agents is provided by the NBC outfit that includes the M17A2 mask, M6A2 hood, and gloves, and the marine is seen drinking through an M1 NBC drinking cap. The weapon is the 5.56-mm (0.22-inch) caliber M16A1 assault rifle.

suppression of antigovernment riots at various times in the 1980s. American relations with Japan, on the other hand, have not undergone the same changes in emphasis, but have deteriorated steadily. There are two reasons. One is the imbalance in American-Japanese trade in favor of the Japanese, and the extraordinary reluctance of the Japanese to shoulder a major part of the defense budget for their own protection and that of Northeast Asia and the western Pacific in general. This burden, the United States feels, should be a basic part of the responsibilities undertaken by an economic superpower such as Japan.

Continued Problems with Japan

These two problems simmered throughout the 1980s as Japan's economic position strengthened still further, but they have not yet reached a

crisis point, as the U.S. is unwilling to put the matters to a decisive test.

The other main consideration in U.S. policy in the Far East is China. After the initial breakthrough secured by President Nixon, President Carter took matters a step farther in December 1978 by "derecognizing" the Republic of China, the state established on Taiwan in 1949 by Generalissimo Chiang Kai-shek after the flight of his Kuomintang party from mainland China at the end of the Chinese Civil War. American recognition switched from Taipei to Peking, and although the move was generally approved in the U.S. for reducing the animosity between the U.S. and China, there were many who condemned Carter's indifferent abandonment of Taiwan. The decision was not reversed by President Reagan, however, though relations with Taiwan were improved at the practical rather than political level despite opposition from the Chinese.

The air operations against Iraq were a multi-nation effort. This SEPECAT Jaguar GR.Mk 1 attack warplane of the British Royal Air Force is about to touch down on a Saudi Arabian airfield after a mission against Iraqi ground targets.

George Bush
For further
references see pages
52, *58*, 59, 62, 76, 79,
81, *82*, *83*, 98, 118,
119, 121, 123

General Dynamics
F-16 Fighting Falcons
of the U.S. Air Force's
363rd Tactical Fighter
Wing, normally based
at Shaw Air Force
Base, South Carolina,
are photographed over
the Persian Gulf with a
Boeing KC-135
Stratotanker of the
Strategic Air
Command.

Under the administration of President George Bush, matters still rest.

A Simpler Middle Eastern Policy

The most volatile of all the regions where there are American interests is the Middle East. The area may not have the grand strategic importance of Europe or even Northeast Asia, but it is the source of most of the world's oil. Therefore, it is very important to U.S. economic interests and of vital importance to the economic interests of the nation's allies, most of whom obtain the bulk of their oil supplies from this bitterly divided region. Yet there is a sharp contrast between the nature of American policy here and in other regions. On one hand, U.S. relations with the U.S.S.R., especially regarding the security of Europe, and to a lesser extent, with the countries of the Far East, have been the subject of bitter controversy in the United States. On the other hand, there has been general agreement in the country about U.S. policy in the Middle East. This policy has three cornerstones: it helps Israel to preserve its independence and security, especially by attempting to bring about a fair settlement of the quarrel between the Israelis and their Arab neighbors; it secures access to the oil of the Persian Gulf at "reasonable prices" for the U.S. and its allies, especially Japan and those in Europe; and it denies the U.S.S.R. "undue influence" in the region.

The true nature of U.S. policy is bedeviled by the need to retain good relations with both the Israelis and the Arabs. This demands an even-handed American approach rather than heavy-handed favoritism; that would alienate one or the other of the mutually antagonistic sides in the bitter Middle Eastern dispute and make it impossible for the U.S. to maintain either the first or the second of its three cornerstones. Therefore there can be no question of an American abandonment of the Israelis, or a U.S. confrontation with the Arab world as a whole.

Fourfold Criteria

The peculiar situation in the Middle East dictates four basic criteria for the U.S. policy toward the Middle East. First, the existence of the Israeli state is not negotiable. Second, while the U.S. is committed to the continued existence of Israel, it is not committed to Israel's existence within specific boundaries. Third, the U.S. wants "normalization" (negotiation) of the conflict between the Israelis and Arabs. Finally, the U.S. seeks to maintain military equality between the two sides.

The Camp David Agreement

It was strictly within the scope of these four basic principles that President Carter achieved the most important foreign affairs success of his administration. The Camp David Agreement finally brought peace between Israel and Egypt and splintered the Arab coalition which had encircled Israel with implacable hostility. It was at best a partial solution to the problem, because it did not address the problems of the Palestinians inside and outside Israel. In the Camp David Agreement, Israel traded the territory it had gained from Egypt in the "Six-Day War" of 1967 for peace on its southwestern frontier. The signature of the Camp David Agreement reduced the threat from the Arab countries. The administration of Israeli Prime Minister Menachem Begin was convinced that the way was now open for a harder line with the Palestinians and an increase in Israeli settlement in the "West Bank," the occupied region of Jordan. With these twin policies, Israel now seemed to be seeking territorial expansion, not peace, in exploiting the political disunity of its enemies to move a step closer to annexing Judea and Samaria.

There was considerable international opposition to this Israeli expansion, but it was verbal rather than effective. Israel therefore felt free to continue its policy against the Palestinians. In 1982, Operation "Peace for Galilee," an Israeli invasion of southern Lebanon, began. It was intended to eliminate the network of

Since its establishment in the aftermath of World War II, the state of Israel had enjoyed a unique relationship with the United States. This photograph, taken in December 1973 shortly after the end of the "Yom Kippur War," shows Secretary of State Dr. Henry Kissinger in conversation with two Israeli leaders, Abba Eban (left) and Yigal Allon.

The Camp David Agreement marked the beginning of major change in the Middle East by ending the threat of war between Israel and Egypt. Seen here with the agreement's broker, President ''Jimmy'' Carter, are Israeli prime minister Menachem Begin (left) and Egyptian president Anwar Sadat.

bases in that war-torn country, which the Palestinians had established as launching pads for operations against northern Israel and the country's seaboard. The whole Israeli policy presented Washington with a difficult dilemma. While the administration of President Reagan supported Israel's right to attack the Palestinian bases used to mount terrorist attacks on Israel, it did not support the wholesale invasion of Lebanon. It also opposed the harsh treatment of Palestinians inside Israel, as well as the establishment of Israeli settlements in the occupied territories.

Intransigent Israel

Israel decided that the time was ripe to pursue its own course. Egypt and Jordan wanted peace, Syria on its own lacked the strength to tackle Israel; Soviet support for the Arabs had waned during a period of preoccupation with events in Afghanistan and Poland; and a world oil surplus had effectively nullified the ''oil weapon'' that the united Arabs had used so effectively against the Western world in 1973. All that the Reagan administration could ask of the Israeli government was a more magnanimous approach to the Palestinian problem, but the Israeli government has consistently

refused. This has strained relations between the U.S. and Israel, but the Israeli government has balanced American interests in the Middle East astutely and therefore retains U.S. support, although it is cooler than it once was.

Problems in the Persian Gulf

Just as the risk of a confrontation between the superpowers over the Arab-Israeli problem waned and eased the situation on the Mediterranean flank of the Middle East, the other flank of the Persian Gulf became increasingly more dangerous, even though it did not offer quite the same threat of superpower confrontation.

The critical point was the overthrow of the imperial regime in Iran in February 1979 and its replacement by an Islamic fundamentalist regime headed by the Ayatollah Khomeini. Under the rule of the Shah Reza Pahlavi, Iran had been an apparently stable and relatively powerful pro-western buffer state between the U.S.S.R. and the other pro-western, but less powerful, states of the Persian Gulf. The U.S. felt able to count on Iran as an anti-Soviet ''regional policeman'' and an effective first-line counter to any Soviet plans for aggression in this vital region. It was a thoroughly convenient situation for

The face of the new Iran, under its fundamentalist Islamic leadership, is chillingly represented by these mullahs (priests) armed with assault rifles.

the U.S., but it changed totally – and virtually overnight – when the Shah was forced to quit his country.

The situation of Iran as an "American surrogate" in the region was not created by President Carter, but it was accepted without criticism and indeed without question when the new president assumed office in January 1977. The administration, the Department of State, and the Department of Defense were taken completely by surprise when the imperial regime collapsed, despite the warning signs provided by increased internal unrest, the manifest corruption of the ruling clique, and the rapid growth of Islamic fundamentalism among the Iranian people as a whole. No contingency plans had been made, and with considerable embarrassment, the administration permitted the ex-Shah to enter the U.S. for treatment of a medical condition that would shortly cause his death. This embarrassment was made all the more shameful because, only a short time before, Carter had publicly praised the Shah as one of the world's greatest leaders.

Thus the departure of the Shah for a short period of exile in another country was greeted with an easily perceptible sense of relief in Washington, and this sent completely the wrong signs to the anti-American regime in Iran. Followers of the new fundamentalist regime took a group of Americans hostage and held them captive in what had been the U.S. embassy in Tehran. The clumsy efforts of the Carter administration to gain their release ended in a bungled military rescue attempt that effectively ended Carter's chances of re-election in the 1980 election. The event meant that Carter was defeated by Reagan, but more importantly, that the first Republican majority in the Senate since 1954 was elected,

Generals of the Imperial Iranian army are seen here before the fall of the Shah in 1979. The United States had high hopes that imperial Iran would be a bastion of stability in the turbulent Middle and Near Eastern regions, but sadly miscalculated the ability of the imperial regime to survive.

Right: Saddam
Hussein

allowing Reagan that freedom to pass legislation that might otherwise have been blocked by a Democratic Congress.

Further Complexities

In itself, the fall of the Iranian imperial regime was a severe blow to American policy in this volatile region. Yet this blow was rapidly followed by two other disastrous episodes; the war between Iraq and Iran, and the Soviet invasion of Afghanistan.

Launched by President Saddam Hussein of Iraq in September 1980, the war had twin objectives. The first was to gain control of the Shatt-al-Arab waterway which then was shared with Iran; the second was to inflict a defeat on the Shi'a Moslem state of Iran to prevent the possibility of Iranian intervention in Iraq, where a Sunni Moslem minority rules the Shi'a Moslem majority.

Iraq achieved some limited successes at the beginning of the war, but was checked by determined Iranian resistance. The war then settled down to a grim conflict of virtually immobile attrition that lasted for 10 incredibly costly years before an armistice was agreed. Throughout this period, the U.S. attempted to remain neutral, for it saw that if either side scored a decisive victory, it could then threaten a more important American ally such as Saudi Arabia. Such a victory could also pose a threat to continued supplies of oil from the Persian Gulf region. The U.S. was not wholly successful in avoiding embroilment in the war, but managed to restrict its involvement to a few small episodes.

Potentially more dangerous was the Soviet involvement in Afghanistan. Here autocratic rule was exercised by Nur Mohammed Taraki, who had come to power with Soviet support in a 1978 coup. Taraki was determined to drag Afghanistan into the 20th century, but his efforts alienated the whole country with the exception of the region around Kabul, the capital. By April 1979, Taraki's regime was facing a nationwide rebellion. The opposition mirrored that which had toppled the imperial regime in Iran just a few months earlier, and the

U.S.S.R. became increasingly worried about the Islamic fundamentalism that now dominated Iran and was making serious dents into Afghanistan. In the longer term, Moscow feared that fundamentalist fervor could spread to the republics of the southern U.S.S.R. unless it was checked. The Soviets urged Taraki to halt his modernization of Afghanistan and to come to an accommodation with those opposing him, but the Afghan president ignored the pleas.

Soviet Military Intervention in Afghanistan

The U.S.S.R. decided that the only solution was military intervention. On the pretext that the Afghan central government had asked for aid in suppressing the rebellion in the outer provinces, the Soviets committed substantial ground forces to Afghanistan during December 1979. The Afghan army put up only a token resistance, and it is estimated that perhaps half of its 80,000 or so men took the opportunity to desert, taking their weapons with them, to join the opposing side's multitude of factional forces.

The result was a small-scale, but exceptionally bitter, irregular war in which the Soviets and a comparatively small Afghan army loyal to the central government fought Moslem guerrilla forces. The opposition groups had safe havens in Pakistan and enjoyed not just the moral, but increasingly, the physical support of the U.S. and some of its allies. This aid gave the guerrillas a small but useful flow of modern weapons such as shoulder-launched surface-to-air missiles, which counterbalanced the Soviets' total air superiority. By the later 1980s, a more practical Soviet administration headed by Mikhail Gorbachev realized that the war in Afghanistan could not be won. In April 1988, Afghanistan and Pakistan signed an agreement, guaranteed by the two superpowers, for the evacuation of all non-Afghan forces by May 1988. With considerable relief, the U.S.S.R. could pull out its forces and leave the Afghans to attempt a settlement of Afghan matters without outside intervention.

The events of February and December 1979 in Iran and Afghanistan finally brought home to the administration that vital American interests in the eastern Middle East were extremely vulnerable. The greater threat seemed to be posed by the Soviet intervention in Afghanistan, which gave the U.S.S.R. several air bases from which their strategic aircraft could roam all over the region and deep into the Indian Ocean. The intervention could also be seen as a possible first step in the fulfillment of a traditional Russian ambition – securing access to a port on the Indian Ocean – by a move into eastern Iran or western Pakistan. It now seems unlikely that such a move was ever part of the Soviet agenda, but at the time the fear of this advance was very real.

Strengthened Forces in the Indian Ocean

After the fall of the Shah, the U.S. Navy had deployed into the northwestern sector of the Indian Ocean various carrier battle groups as well as an amphibious squadron of between four and six ships carrying a marine amphibious unit (a battalion landing team, a composite aircraft squadron, and a service support unit totaling 2,350 marine and 156 naval personnel). It was recognized

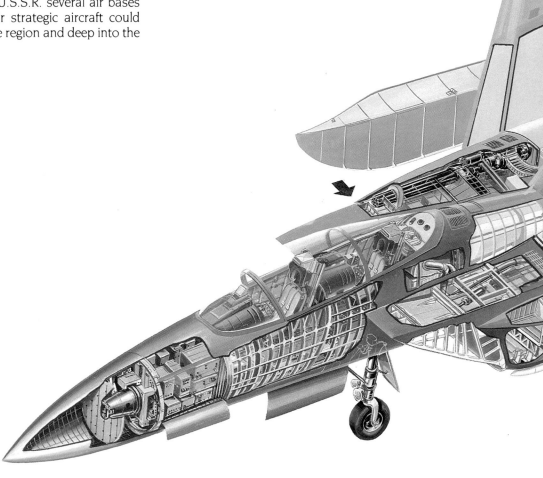

One of the most versatile warplanes that the U.S. Air Force deployed to Saudi Arabia for the war with Iraq was the McDonnell Douglas F-15 Eagle, which first flew in July 1972. Designed as a successor to the same company's legendary F-4 Phantom II multirole fighter, it is optimized for the air-superiority role but, like the General Dynamics F-16 Fighting Falcon, it has matured as a true multirole plane with important attack capability. The Eagle has an advanced structure and carefully blended aerodynamics for great strength and low drag. The latter combines with the powerful engines to provide this large fighter with sparkling flight performance, including the ability to climb vertically when not heavily loaded. The F-15A single-seat and F-15B two-seat versions entered service in November 1974 with a powerplant of two 23,830-pound (10,809-kg) afterburning thrust Pratt & Whitney F100-P-100 turbofans, but the versions delivered since June 1979 have been the F-15C single-seater and F-15D two-seater, the latter retaining full combat capability. The two models' improvements over the F-15A and F-15B include updated and more versatile APG-70 radar, slightly less powerful 23,450-pound (10,637-kg) afterburning thrust F100-P-220 turbofans with a digital control system for greater operational flexibility, and provision for so-called FAST (Fuel And Sensor, Tactical) packs. The plane illustrated is the latest F-15E, a development of the F-15D as a two-seat interdictor and strike warplane capable of day and night operations in all weather conditions when fitted with the LANTIRN podded low-level navigation and targeting system.

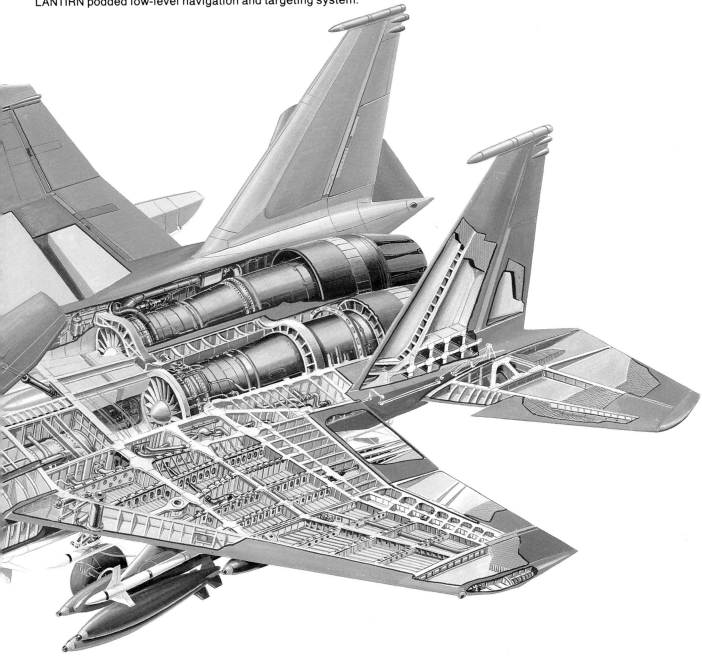

Opposite: Tugs nudge the battleship U.S.S. *Wisconsin* against a pier at the Ingalls Shipbuilding facility of Litton Industries at Pascagoula, Mississippi, during January 1987. The ship had just been towed from New Orleans, Louisiana, for "demothballing" and modernization before being recommissioned into the U.S. Navy's active fleet.

that the real capability offered by this force was small. Within weeks of the Soviet move into Afghanistan, President Carter therefore responded by announcing plans to develop a task force designed to give the U.S. the ability to respond rapidly to any crisis in the area. In March 1980, the Department of Defense established the headquarters of the so-called Rapid Deployment Joint Task Force. At the same time Department of State began the laborious task of negotiating with the regional powers to win base facilities in the area, but most countries soon proved themselves less willing to treat with the U.S. than they had been with the Shah.

The RDJTF was planned from the beginning to provide the U.S. with the capability to intervene in local crises, but also to be able to tackle the most serious (but in fact the least likely) opponent, namely Soviet conventional forces. The rationale of this planning, whose validity has always been suspect, was that the ability to deal with the "worst-case scenario" (combat with Soviet conventional forces) necessarily meant an ability to cope with the lesser threat posed by regional forces.

Possible Opposition

The planners at the Department of Defense looked first at the Soviet forces in the three military districts bordering northern Iran. Here, the North Caucasus, Transcaucasus, and Turkestan Military Districts controlled 24 divisions (one airborne, one tank, and 22 motor rifle), most of them, except the airborne division, at the lowest level of readiness with only some 25 percent of their troops up to full strength and a comparatively high percentage of obsolete or obsolescent equipment. The American planners concluded that the Soviets would need three to four weeks for full mobilization in the region, giving the corresponding U.S. forces that time scale to get into position and receive their equipment.

The American planners reckoned that the Soviet divisions would be supported by about 450 combat aircraft of the two air armies flanking the Caspian Sea. Like

Rapid Deployment Joint Task Force
For further references
see pages
26, 27, 28, 30

their ground force counterparts, the air armies had a fairly high percentage of obsolescent aircraft. But even the presence of large numbers of advanced warplanes, such as the Sukhoi Su-24 "Flanker" interdictor assumed in the "worst-case scenario," gave the Soviets the ability to operate only to the extreme northern end of the Persian Gulf.

An extra factor was added to the equation by the Soviet forces in Afghanistan, thought to number 100,000 troops and substantial air support elements. American planners had to take into account the possibility of a Soviet offensive from Afghanistan across the comparatively flat eastern plateau of Iran to the Strait of Hormuz at the southern entrance to the Persian Gulf. Such an offensive would have offered several operational advantages, but was thought unlikely because of the scale of operations in Afghanistan and the threat to their lines of communication if the Soviets struck off into Iran. The most likely use of Afghanistan, it was reckoned, was as a forward "aircraft carrier" from which Soviet strategic medium bombers such as the Tupolev Tu-26 "Backfire" could strike deep into the Indian Ocean.

American planners also knew that the single airborne divisions based north of Iran and in Afghanistan could be reinforced at short notice by one or more of the eight airborne divisions that were controlled directly from Moscow and constituted the U.S.S.R.'s main rapid-deployment force. The American planners bore in mind that airborne forces had spearheaded the Soviet moves into Czechoslovakia in 1968 and Afghanistan in 1979, and they felt confident that any new Soviet adventure would start with an airborne operation, with troops being airlifted to distant locations and then moving out in their own specialized transport and armored fighting vehicles.

Significant Airlift Capability

If the Soviet military airlift capability was used solely for the movement of airborne forces, it could transport two whole divisions simultaneously, with the civil capacity of Aeroflot available for the

delivery of part of a third division. American planners took this into account when deciding that the Soviets would be able to project two divisions to a range of 600 miles, or one division to 1,000 miles, or a smaller force to a greater range if intermediate bases were held for refueling.

Finally, there was the Soviet navy. American planners were confident that it would play only a subsidiary role in any Middle Eastern adventure. In theory the Soviet naval infantry (marines) offered some capability, but the possibility of its use in this region was discounted as the naval infantry had been designed for European operations. In any case, the Soviet navy lacked the capability to support ship-landed forces so far from their bases. It was anticipated, however, that Soviet surface warships might attack U.S. Navy forces moving into the Persian Gulf, and that Soviet submarines

might harass American shipping in the Strait of Hormuz.

The Rapid Deployment Joint Task Force...

With such Soviet forces and capabilities in mind, the American planners felt that there was no need to create new formations for the RDJTF. It was therefore allocated one marine amphibious force, three army divisions, a number of smaller combat and support units, and seven tactical fighter wings of the U.S. Air Force and Air National Guard. One composite carrier task force with ships was provided by three carrier task forces of the U.S. Navy's 6th and 7th Fleets, located in the Mediterranean and western Pacific respectively. The U.S. Marine Corps' contribution was a composite formation made up of elements from I and II

Crewmen on board the assault ship U.S.S. *Nassau* prepare to refuel two McDonnell Douglas AV-8B Harrier II warplanes as a third machine prepares to land. The ability of these aircraft to take off with a heavy load of weapons and fuel after a very short run, and then to land vertically after expending their weapons and fuel, allows them to operate from many types of ship, as well as makeshift airstrips on shore.

The need for additional firepower in regions such as the Middle East was one of the reasons why the administration of President Ronald Reagan decided to reactivate the four World War II battleships of the "Iowa" class, represented here by the U.S.S. *New Jersey* underway shortly after her recommissioning, with the "Knox" class frigate U.S.S. *Meyerkord*. Well armored and fitted with exceptionally heavy gun armament, the "Iowa" class battleships were ideally suited for supporting amphibious operations, while their extensive command and communication facilities made them very capable command ships for task forces.

Marine Amphibious Forces. It included one marine division with an aircraft wing and a command support group (in all, some 48,200 marine and 2,400 navy personnel carried in about 50 amphibious ships). The army element was XVIII Airborne Corps (the 82nd Airborne and 101st Airmobile Divisions) reinforced by the 24th Mechanized Division. These formations amounted to some 200,000 men. With the exception of the last, all these marine and army formations were of the "light" type, with only limited capability against Soviet tank and even motorized rifle divisions. The contributions of the USAF and ANG totaled about 500 tactical warplanes.

...becomes Central Command

After considerable debate and early experience, the RDJTF was elevated to the

To escort and protect its valuable nuclear-powered aircraft carriers, the U.S. Navy produced several classes of nuclear-powered cruisers. This is the U.S.S. *Arkansas*, one of the four-strong "Virginia" class. Its nuclear powerplant provides effectively unlimited endurance, which has distinct operational advantages. It also removes the need for fuel storage on board, with more room to carry weapons.

status of a unified command on January 1, 1983, and renamed Central Command, with its headquarters in Florida. The commander was to be provided by the army and marine corps on an alternating basis. As the head of a unified command, the commander reported directly to the Secretary of Defense. However, the U.S. Navy retained direct control of its ships and of the assigned marine units until they were actually landed. They then came under the control of Central Command, whose Forward Headquarters Element was located with the headquarters of the U.S. Navy's commander of the

Middle East force at Manama in Bahrain.

The importance attached to Central Command grew rapidly, and within 12 months, it had reached a strength of two marine and five army divisions, supported by the equivalent of 10 tactical air wings.

The command arrangements were controversial from the beginning of Central Command's existence. Some of the controversy arose from the politics and personalities associated with the command, while other aspects of the controversy stemmed from the reluctance of the services to lose most of the strategic flexibility left to them after the removal of

Although the U.S. Marine Corps uses many of the weapons and much of the equipment of the U.S. Army, the corps' dedication to the fast-reaction and amphibious roles requires a certain number of specialized items. Typical of these is the LAV-25, or Light Armored Vehicle 25-mm cannon, which entered service in 1983 as a multirole type. The LAV-25 has a checkered design and development history; it is an 8 × 8 (eight wheels, all powered) derivative of a Canadian 6 × 6 vehicle, the Grizzly, produced by General Motors Canada as the armored personnel carrier version of the AVGP (Armored Vehicle General Purpose) series, itself evolved from a Swiss type, the MOWAG Piranha. The LAV series itself includes a number of specialized variants, but this LAV-25 is basically an armored personnel carrier, with attributes of the infantry fighting vehicle since it possesses powerful turreted armament. The LAV-25 carries nine men – three crewmen and six infantrymen, the latter provided with two rear doors and two roof hatches.

forces earmarked for NATO: in the case of the U.S. Army, for instance, the five divisions earmarked to Central Command constituted almost all of its strategic reserve. Another element of the controversy came from the services' different operational approach to crisis management: in the case of the U.S. Navy, for example, the reluctance to tie any of its forces to Central Command was the inevitable consequence of its view that in times of crisis naval operations should be considered on a global rather than regional scale.

Such command and organizational problems were simple, however, by comparison with the difficulty of moving the men and all their equipment to their operational area. For 20 years, the U.S. military establishment had effectively ignored the problem of strategic lift, the mass movement of men and materiel over considerable distances in the shortest possible time. This physical limitation was compounded by the reluctance of the ''friendly'' states of the Persian Gulf to allow the establishment of U.S. bases, and also by the fears of the administration that attempts to create the bases as bastions of stability in these states might

NATO
For further references see pages
30, 33, 36, 48, 50, 53

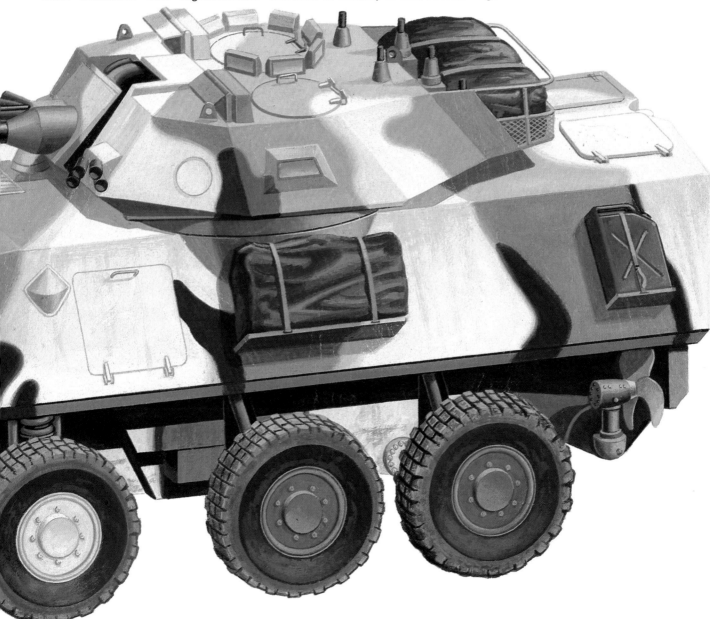

actually destabilize the host states by giving anti-American sentiment something on which to build.

Limited Sea and Air Lift Capabilities

At the time of the RDJTF's creation, the U.S. had no fast sealift capability. Airlift capability could move only one battalion of the 82nd Airborne Division to the Persian Gulf in two days and one brigade in two weeks, and to move the whole division would take a month. Even this poor capacity was based on the assumption that none of the air power would be diverted for tasks such as the movement of vital basing equipment.

The rationale behind the RDJTF and Central Command was the prepositioning of equipment (vehicles, heavy weapons, ammunition, fuel, spares, and all the other paraphernalia of modern war) close to the anticipated scene of action. There they could be collected, checked, and taken away by troops as they arrived by air and sea.

The Persian Gulf states were reluctant to accept such prepositioned stores or the small numbers of troops needed to guard and maintain them. The only two regional points of access open to the Department of Defense were the NATO base at Incirlik in southeastern Turkey and the Indian Ocean island of Diego Garcia, 2,000 miles from the Persian Gulf in the Chagos Archipelago of the British Indian Ocean Territory. Neither of these bases had any prepositioned stores for incoming troops, and the only naval support for the ground forces was provided by one or two carrier battle groups. The single group operating in the waters of what the Department of Defense planners called Southwest Asia had been increased to two during 1979, but had since reverted to a single group occasionally supplemented by a second group.

Boosting Military Airlift Command...

An essential first step was therefore a major improvement in the size and overall efficiency of the U.S. strategic lift capability. An initial boost was provided by the USAF program that by 1982 had "stretched" the Lockheed Star-Lifter logistic transport by converting the original C-141As into 279 C-141Bs with a longer fuselage and inflight-refueling capability. Further capability was provided by the accelerated purchase of 60 McDonnell Douglas KC-10A Extender tanker/transports. Between 1982 and 1988, 50 C-5B versions of the Lockheed Galaxy strategic transport were procured, boosting the capacity of the heavy freight fleet by some 60 percent. From 1980, a major diplomatic effort secured refueling rights for these and other aircraft in several European countries, as well as Morocco and Egypt, on the most direct air route from the U.S. to the Persian Gulf.

Such aircraft are useful only for the rapid movement of light loads such as men. The movement of heavy equipment in large quantities required ships and, in the absence of bases on friendly soil, equipment stored on prepositioned ships. Over much the same period, therefore, the U.S. Navy made a considerable effort directed along two main lines.

...and Military Sealift Command

In May 1980, several U.S. ports saw the loading of ships with equipment and munitions for the U.S. Marine Corps. These ships, both transports of the Military Sealift Command and contracted merchant tonnage, were in position at Diego Garcia by the middle of July as the first element of the Near-Term Prepositioning Force (NTPF). The ships were two vessels already in MSC service, two more acquired for the task, and three merchant vessels. In all, these seven ships carried enough equipment, ammunition, spare parts, fuel, food, and water to support a marine amphibious brigade (a regimental landing team, a composite aircraft group, and a brigade service support group totaling 15,000 marine and 670 naval personnel carried in anything between 21 and 26 amphibious

All of the aircraft carriers built for the U.S. Navy since the end of World War II remain in service as warships that have been maintained at a level of exceptional offensive power by modernization and improvement programs. Typical of the first-generation ships, before the advent of nuclear power, is the U.S.S. *Ranger*, one of the four-strong "Forrestal" class. The ship was commissioned in August 1957 and has a full-load displacement of 81,165 tons. Four sets of geared steam turbines deliver 280,000 horsepower to four shafts for a maximum speed of 34 knots, and range is 9,200 miles at 20 knots. The ship carries its own crew of 160 officers and 2,730 enlisted troops, in addition to the air group section of 290 officers and 2,190 enlisted personnel, for a maximum capacity of 90 aircraft launched and handled with the aid of four steam catapults and four deck-edge lifts.

ships, and several USAF tactical squadrons) for two weeks of sustained operations. As time progressed, some of these ships were replaced, and at the end of 1983 the NTPF contained six ships for the marine amphibious brigade, three ships loaded with ammunition for Central Command's army element, one ship carrying medical supplies (including two 400-bed army field hospitals and one 200-bed combat support hospital), and seven ships carrying fuel and water. Another prepositioned ship was located in the Mediterranean during the same period.

The NTPF was essentially an interim measure for one marine amphibious brigade, which could be put ashore in about 48 hours (but only through fairly well equipped ports in a friendly state).

The Definitive MPS Program

The navy's longer-term plan was based on support for three marine amphibious brigades (45,000 men) using 13 special Maritime Prepositioning Ships (MPS), of which five were built for the task and the other eight converted to it. The MPS force was phased in from 1984, with four ships supporting one marine amphibious brigade, rising to nine ships supporting two brigades in 1985, and finally to 13 ships supporting three brigades in 1986. The stocks on the ships were designed to allow three brigades to undertake 30 days of sustained operations, and the ships were designed to move the equipment of the three brigades (one marine division) ashore using their own unloading equipment. The arrival of the last MPS allowed the final six NTPF ships to be pulled out of Diego Garcia in 1987.

In both the NTPF and MPS "eras," it was assumed that the troops would be airlifted to their operational region and meet their equipment in that region. Before the troops could meet their equipment, the planes needed overflying and refueling rights, and secure airfields linked by road to the ports and/or other areas where the equipment would be unloaded. The prepositioned ships would have to sail from Diego Garcia to the port/airfield complex near the planned operational area and would be vulnerable to air, sea, and submarine attack during this journey, so naval escort was essential. At their destination, the ships needed a safe anchorage and unloading piers. The 327 amphibious tractors carried by the ships offered only a modest capability and were actually planned for ground transport, not for amphibious movement or assault. Thus the successful link-up between the airlifted troops and their sealifted equipment demanded at best a friendly (or at least a nonantagonistic) state offering the right airfield/port combination. This state had to be close to the planned operational area; the marines and their equipment could not be reembarked in the prepositioning ships even for transit, let alone assault.

The U.S. Navy decided that it needed additional rapid-response capability and bought eight SL-7-type fast merchant carriers for conversion into roll-on/roll-off transports to fill the vehicle/cargo fast-response role. These ships were conceived mainly for use in connection with Central Command operations, but not earmarked for its exclusive support. They are based as groups of four ships on the east and west coasts for maximum flexibility of response. The ships were ready by 1985 and provided the capability to move one armored or mechanized division from the U.S. to the Southwest Asia region via the Cape of Good Hope in less than three weeks, excluding the 10 days needed to load and unload the ships.

Support from the Ready Reserve Force

It was anticipated that the NTPF and MPS tonnage, supported by the rapid-response ships, would suffice to get U.S. forces into action quickly and support them in the short term with all essential supplies. Follow-on materiel and other supplies would then be brought in by ships of the Ready Reserve Force, merchant vessels laid up under the control of the Maritime Administration. The ships, including some with special provision for carrying military equipment, are moth-balled at a high state of readiness and can be prepared for use within a few days. In 1983 the RRF numbered 30 merchant vessels, although the goal of an ambitious program to improve sealift was a total of 77 ships (61 dry cargo ships and 16 tankers). Some of the ships were modified as auxiliary crane ships with heavy lifting equipment. They can unload their own and other ships' cargoes and thus do without the extensive (and therefore vulnerable) port facilities that would otherwise be essential.

Weapons in Saudi Arabia...

Another aspect of the prepositioning program was the location of U.S. Army war stocks at Diego Garcia. There was a possibility of further stocks at Masirah in Oman and Ras Banas in Egypt, and the air force planned to build dumps of munitions and spares at both places. The U.S. also used its arms transfer policy as an alternative to prepositioning, especially in the case of the high-technology systems provided to Saudi Arabia. According to the 1982 deal covering the sale of five Boeing E-3 Sentry airborne warning and control system aircraft to Saudi Arabia, the U.S. had access to information from these aircraft even after they had been delivered and taken under Saudi control. Saudi Arabia also bought larger quantities of air-to-air and air-to-surface weapons than it needed for its force of McDonnell Douglas F-15 Eagle multirole fighters, which would also be available to USAF fighters deployed to the region. Another important advantage for American aircraft and vehicles operating in this region was the ready availability of fuel from local stocks. The two bases at which the highest concentration of weapons and fuel was to be found were those at Dhahran and in King Khaled Military City, giving American warplanes simple access to the Persian Gulf and to the area of the northern Gulf and the Iran/Iraq frontier respectively.

All this depended, of course, on the willingness of the Saudi government to give U.S. warplanes access to Saudi bases. This was in no way guaranteed,

Opposite: In the period from the end of World War II to the beginning of the 1990s, the main strategic preoccupation of the American forces was Europe, which would probably have been the flashpoint of any World War III between the U.S.S.R. and its Warsaw Pact satellites against the forces of the North Atlantic Treaty Organization. Most American tactical weapons were therefore planned with this primary theater in mind, and the McDonnell Douglas Helicopter (originally Hughes) AH-64 Apache was no exception. Seen here during a typical training sortie in Germany, the Apache was planned as an antitank helicopter for European operations, and in addition to its suite of advanced avionics and sensors for all-weather day/night operational capability, it has a very potent armament. Under the fuselage is a remote-controlled 30-mm cannon used for the suppression of ground fire, and on the four hardpoints under the stub wings is the offensive armament, in this instance eight AGM-114 Hellfire laser-guided antitank missiles and two launchers, each carrying nineteen 2.75-inch (70-mm) air-to-surface rockets.

but was the subject of unwritten understandings. The fact that the Saudis and Americans shared the same concerns about Iran and Iraq made it extremely unlikely that such access would be denied. To a lesser extent, this problem also affected the possibility of American use of bases in other Persian Gulf states and even in Egypt. In an effort to reduce the possible effect of an Arab refusal to grant access to American warplanes and ships, the U.S. negotiated "contingency access rights" to airfields and ports in Oman, Somalia, and Kenya. The successful negotiation of these rights went a considerable way to easing the potential problems that could otherwise be faced by naval support and rapid deployment forces.

...and Expanded Facilities in Turkey

In the fall of 1982, and within the context of a larger package of aid and arms connected with Turkey's vital position on NATO's southeastern flank, the U.S. reached agreement with the Turkish government for basing rights in eastern Turkey. The U.S. was allowed to create NATO bases at Konya, Van, and Kars. Because all three lay close to the Soviet frontier, it was anticipated that they would have to be provided with strong defenses, as well as considerable construction and stocks, before they could be of significant value. Turkey also insisted that the bases be reserved for NATO use rather than U.S. commitments in the Persian Gulf.

Huge Tasks and Limited Resources

In 1986, the U.S. Army had 522,850 men in the continental U.S.A. Three and a half divisions were "double-earmarked" to NATO and to Central Command. Given the world problems of the time, the need for something like Central Command was

33

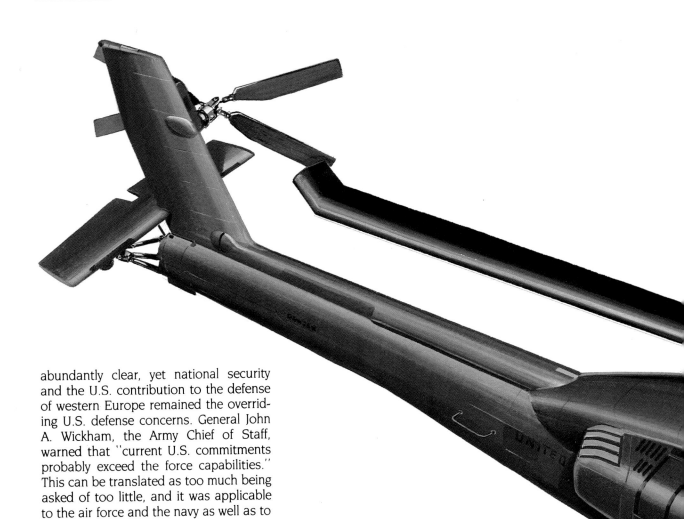

abundantly clear, yet national security and the U.S. contribution to the defense of western Europe remained the overriding U.S. defense concerns. General John A. Wickham, the Army Chief of Staff, warned that "current U.S. commitments probably exceed the force capabilities." This can be translated as too much being asked of too little, and it was applicable to the air force and the navy as well as to the army.

During the 1980s, therefore, the U.S. forces thought long and hard about their basic natures and organizations with a view to improving their operational capabilities, especially regarding the need for American power to be projected abroad.

Army planners came to the early conclusion that its formations had to be structured for possible deployment anywhere in the world. This decision raised problems of maintaining full operational capability in widely different areas, terrains, and even types of warfare. Given the technological and numerical realities of the situation, U.S. forces could not hope to win any campaign by remaining on the operational defensive and using attrition as a major "weapon." In addition, while the army had to be organized and equipped to win on the conventional battlefield, it also to had possess the

The most important battlefield helicopter operated by the U.S. Army is the McDonnell Douglas AH-64A Apache, a large yet powerful type that has high performance and a surprising level of agility at low level. The pilot occupies the raised rear seat, and the gunner is in the front seat, where he has an excellent view of the country ahead and to the sides of the helicopter's flight path. The type is powered by two 1,696-horsepower (1,265-kW) General Electric T700-GE-701 turboshafts and has a maximum takeoff weight of 21,000 pounds (9,525 kg) with a maximum 3,880-pound (1,760-kg) weapon load. The maximum speed is 184 miles per hour (296 km/h), and the dimensions include a main rotor diameter of 48 feet (14.63 m) and an overall length of 48 feet 2 inches (14,68 m) with the rotors turning.

capability to survive, and then to respond to, any first use of nuclear, biological, and chemical weapons by an enemy.

"AirLand Battle 2000"

These corollaries resulted in two efforts that have had a great effect on the nature of the army. The first was a new tactical doctrine, the so-called "AirLand Battle 2000" concept, and the other a change in the army's organization to accord with the new tactical doctrine and the weapons associated with it. Before looking at these aspects, however, it is useful to consider the basic elements of the AirLand Battle 2000 concept.

The core of the new concept was derived from a 20-year assessment of the nature and possible development of the Soviet threat in Europe The United States and its European allies would be outnumbered in personnel and equipment. In these circumstances, a defensive war of attrition would probably not succeed, so another basic operational method was needed The best possibilities seemed to be offered by a strategic defense of the NATO central region through aggressive tactics involving immediate, sustained, and simultaneous attacks on the line of contact with the enemy and in the depth of the enemy's rear areas. This offensive defense would be undertaken by striking quickly at the Soviet first echelons while locating the follow-on echelons. The object was to fix and destroy the first echelons before the follow-on echelons could intervene and tip the balance of power in favor of the soviets.

This meant that the Soviet assault forces (first and follow-on echelons) should be attacked throughout the depth of their position by high-mobility forces using armor, artillery, air, and electronic weapons. This tactic was designed to confuse the Soviets and make them fight in more than one direction by deploying maneuver forces in the rear of their first echelons, during the interval of time and space between the first and follow-on echelons. Such a riposte would destroy the cohesion of the Soviets' timetable and force them to change their plans in such matters as altering lines of advance and splitting forces.

A Battlefield Scenario

The whole concept was based on high levels of training and the availability of high-technology systems, especially in communications, for the rapid collection and assessment of intelligence information.

The AirLand Battle 2000 concept, put forward in 1982, can be neatly summarized as winning the initiative right at the beginning of the battle. It was based on inherently aggressive tactics using high levels of maneuverability and a perceptive recognition of human factors on the battlefield. Within the overall concept, there were four main aspects. First there was initiative, to make the enemy react to the U.S. forces, not the other way around. Second, there was depth, a three-dimensional combination of time, distance, and resources, to provide flexibility in defense and momentum in attack. Third, there was agility, not only in the physical sense of "getting there firstest with the mostest," but also in the speed and flexibility of planning and decision-making. Finally, there was synchronization, a total unity of effort across the operational board.

The conduct of a successful offensive defense would pave the way for large-scale offensive operations. These would be based on the five well-established principles: concentration in space and time to achieve significant superiority over the enemy; surprise, so that the offensive hit the enemy's weak spot; speed, so that the enemy was put off balance and kept that way; flexibility, so that opportunities could be exploited as and when they arose; and audacity, so that operations were conducted with a recognition of risk, but without undue gambling.

Within these defensive and offensive concepts, the basic organizational formation was the army. It was not altered essentially by the adoption of the AirLand Battle 2000 concept, but its subordinate elements were modified quite considerably.

Among the possible horrors of the modern battlefield could be nuclear, biological, and chemical (NBC) weapons. To counter this threat, modern armies have special suits designed to provide the wearer with filtered air while preventing any airborne agent from reaching his skin. This marine is wearing NBC gear.

The corps, of which two or more were grouped together to create an army, became the fundamental maneuver formation at command and logistical level. The two types of corps envisaged were the heavy corps controlling between three and two-thirds divisions and five divisions, and a corps controlling between two divisions and three and two-thirds divisions, which would possess at least 60,000 personnel and be capable of expansion as necessary.

Considerable provision was also made within the "AirLand Battle 2000" concept for a far tighter and more wider-ranging integration between U.S. and allied forces than had been contemplated before.

Divisional Structure

The army's active ground combat force contained 16 divisions. The division is the largest formation that trains and enters combat as a combined-arms team.

Most of the officers who eventually reach high rank in the U.S. Army are products of the U.S. Military Academy at West Point, New York, where all types of training, including operations on water, are standard.

Therefore, it is a balanced fighting team able to sustain operations for some time without support from other army elements. Its self-sustaining nature also makes the division suitable for a number of independent roles, especially when supported by specially attached combat support and combat service support elements. Despite this capability for independent operations, however, the division generally operates within the framework of a corps command. In Division '86 form, the division was organized to fight anywhere in the world, and to undertake conventional operations, or operations that combined the conventional with nuclear, biological, and chemical aspects.

The 16 divisions of the ground combat force were provided from the 18 divisions of the active army's major maneuver forces. These included four armored divisions, six infantry divisions, five light divisions, one air assault division, one airborne division, and one high-technology motorized infantry division. The reserve component (Army Reserve and Army National Guard) added another 10 divisions in the form of two armored divisions, five infantry divisions, two mechanized divisions, and one light division.

Other Maneuver Units

Below this formation level, the army could also call on a large number of nondivisional maneuver units at brigade level. In the active army, there was one armored brigade, one infantry brigade, one air cavalry combat brigade, four Special Forces groups, one Delta Force, and one assault brigade, a total of nine brigade-sized units. In the reserve component, the nondivisional maneuver units were three armored brigades, seven mechanized brigades, 10 infantry brigades, and four Special Forces groups, a total of 19 brigade-sized nondivisional maneuver units.

Within the division – the standard combined-arms formation – the basic maneuver unit was the battalion. The division was organized on the basis of three brigades, and each of these three headquarters was allocated between three and five battalions at the discretion of the divisional commander. The headquarters of the cavalry brigade (air attack) could also command ground forces, which in effect gave the division a fourth brigade.

Heavy maneuver battalions (armor and mechanized infantry) are best suited to operations in open country in any part of the world and are designed to use open terrain to maximum operational and tactical advantage. Light maneuver battalions (rifle infantry, air assault infantry, and ranger infantry) are better suited to operations in tighter country where close fighting can be undertaken.

Thus, the division's maneuver units were grouped under brigade command according to the dictates of the terrain, the opposition, and the mission to be undertaken. Armored and mechanized infantry units were rarely designed to fight in isolation, but were grouped in brigades so that the armored battalions would offset the infantry battalions' weaknesses, and vice versa. This arrangement allowed the brigade and divisional commanders to exploit the strengths of the two types of battalion to maximum effect. At a slightly lower organizational level, a battalion task force included armored and mechanized infantry companies in a balance designed to meet a specific need: a force heavy in armor would be formed for open-country operations, a force heavy in mechanized infantry for fighting in closer country or urban situations, and an evenly balanced force for mixed country or in conditions where reconnaisance was sketchy.

Multiple Capabilities for All Conditions

The different types of division were designed to provide the army with formations suitable for conditions that might be encountered anywhere in the world. Given the army's responsibility for rapid reaction to crisis in any part of the world, the light division was the logical

Cadets on a patrol exercise. Like all training, such exercises are made as realistic as possible right from the beginning of the training period. The object is to fix in the cadet's mind that this is no game, but the kind of practice that may well preserve his life in the future.

solution to the need for a highly transportable formation. The light division generally had a strength of 17,000 officers and troops and, with ease of transportation in mind, was configured for capability against enemy tanks by nonarmored means. This meant very limited – or indeed no – organic tank units, with antitank capability provided by specialized missiles, such as the TOW with its launcher carried on a light armored vehicle or another high-mobility type.

The light division had nine or 10 infantry battalions, together with support elements comparable to those of the heavy division, but scaled down to lighter weapons and reduced capabilities. Of the 16 divisions of the army's ground combat force, it was planned that 10 would be heavy and the other six light (four infantry, one airborne, and one air-mobile).

Included among the basic units were the tank battalion, the mechanized infantry battalion, the cavalry brigade (air attack), and the divisional artillery. The tank battalion numbered 565 officers and troops organized into a headquarters company and four tank companies. The headquarters company included the battalion's maintenance and support elements, a scout platoon, and a mortar platoon with six weapons. Each tank company numbered three platoons, each with four M60 tanks, for a battalion strength of 48 main battle tanks. The organization was slightly modified with the advent of the M1 Abrams tank, and current tank battalions have a total of 58 main battle tanks.

Tank Battalions: The Task

The function of such tank battalions is to use their mobility to outflank the enemy, or to exploit their firepower to break through the enemy's main defenses. On reaching the enemy's rear areas, they should destroy or at least disrupt the depth of the enemy's position and make

One of the most important tactical weapons in current service with the American forces is the TOW (Tube launched, Optically tracked, Wire guided) antitank missile. More formally known as the BGM-71, this heavyweight, but portable, missile system has been produced in vast numbers for the U.S. and allied forces. The missile has been steadily upgraded in overall capabilities and in its latest versions is thought to be able to defeat the protection of even the latest main battle tanks.

the task of the follow-up forces easier. Tank forces are also ideally suited to exploiting any breach in the enemy's defenses with a dynamic pursuit.

Mechanized Infantry Battalions: The Task

The mechanized infantry battalion had a strength of 880 officers and men organized into one headquarters company, one antiarmor company, and four mechanized rifle companies. Both the tank and mechanized infantry battalions had a basic four-company structure, so it was easy to switch companies to create tank and mechanized infantry battalion task forces. As in the tank battalion, maintenance and support elements were grouped within the headquarters company, which also included a scout platoon and a mortar platoon. The antiarmor company had 12 Improved TOW Vehicles, each one an armored

personnel carrier fitted with an elevating launcher for the TOW heavyweight antitank missile and provision for reloading missiles in the hull. The men of each mechanized rifle company were carried in the M113 armored personnel carrier (now being replaced by the M2 Bradley Infantry Fighting Vehicle), and each company was also provided with nine Dragon portable antitank missile launchers.

The mechanized infantry generally operated as part of a combined-arms task force. The infantrymen remained in their IFVs for the mobile phase of the operation and dismounted only when forced to do so by the enemy or if the operation became static. In this latter situation, the infantry dismounted and undertook an assault designed to shift the enemy and restore mobility to the battlefield. In this role, the M2 IFV offers considerably greater capabilities than the M113. The earlier vehicle had good mobility and protection, but only very limited support capability from its 0·5-in (12·7-mm)

One of the most important battlefield air-defense weapons fielded by the U.S. Army is the M163. One of many systems based on the chassis and automotive system of the M113 armored personnel carrier, it is basically that vehicle with its hull-top adapted to accommodate the weapon mounting of the M167 towed equipment.

cupola-mounted heavy machine gun; the later vehicle provides better mobility (comparable with that of the M1 Abrams tank), superior protection, and an altogether more formidable level of supporting fire from its 25-mm turret-mounted cannon and retractable twin-tube launcher for seven TOW missiles.

Air Support for the Ground Forces

The cavalry brigade (air attack) had a strength of some 1,700 officers and troops, and was designed to control the division's air assets, as well as providing a fourth brigade headquarters for ground operations. Controlled by a headquarters troop, the cavalry brigade (air attack) deployed two attack helicopter battalions, a combat support aviation battalion, and the divisional cavalry squadron. Each attack helicopter battalion had 21 McDonnell Douglas AH-64A Apache battlefield helicopters and 13 Bell OH-58C Kiowa scout helicopters (now being replaced by the more capable OH-58D Aeroscout version). The combat

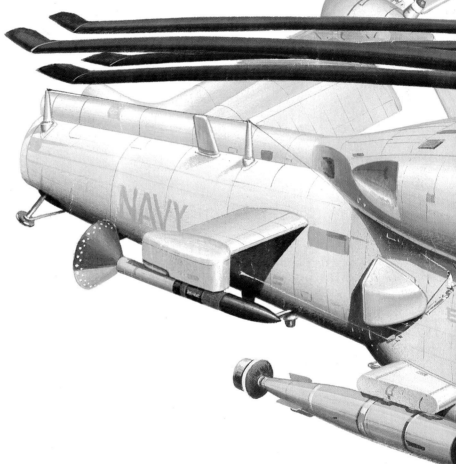

One of the most important antisubmarine "weapons" carried by major surface warships of the U.S. Navy is the Sikorsky SH-60B Seahawk, a naval adaptation of the UH-60 Black Hawk utility helicopter. The type was developed as the LAMPS Mk III (Light Airborne Multi-Purpose System Mk III) to replace the LAMPS Mk I (Kaman SH-2F Seasprite), and differs from its land-based counterpart in having a folding main rotor, a folding tail, revised landing gear, a haul-down system for recovery onto pitching decks, and a different electronic system that includes search radar, an electronic support measures system, a magnetic anomaly detection system using an orange and red towed sensor "bird" stowed on the starboard side of the rear fuselage, and on the port side of the fuselage a 25-round pneumatic launcher for 125 sonobuoys.

support aviation battalion included 30 helicopters for utility tasks, but the most important machines were six Sikorsky EH-60 Black Hawk helicopters with electronic warfare systems to intercept and jam the enemy's all-important communications network. The divisional cavalry squadron contained four troops, two of them heliborne and the other two carried in a derivative of the M2 Bradley, the M3 Cavalry Fighting Vehicle. The two air cavalry troops each controlled four Apaches and six Kiowas, and the two ground cavalry troops each deployed 20 CFVs. These latter have provision for two rather than the IFV's seven embarked infantrymen, with the empty internal volume used to carry considerably more ammunition (1,500 rather than 900 25-mm cannon rounds, 4,540 rather than 2,340 0·3-in/ 7·62-mm machine gun rounds, and 12, not seven, TOW missiles).

The Kiowa (or Aeroscout) and Apache teams offer formidable capabilities. The light and nimble OH-58 moves ahead of the more heavily armed AH-64 to find and report targets, which the Apache then acquires with its advanced sensors and

engages with weapons that include a 30-mm cannon for the suppression of ground fire, up to 16 Hellfire missiles for the destruction of tanks, and multi-tube launchers for 2·75-in (70-mm) air-to-surface rockets.

Divisional Artillery

The divisional artillery, with some 3,000 officers and troops on its strength, was designed along traditional lines, providing both short-range fire support (direct and indirect) for the division's maneuver units and longer-range fire support for U.S. and allied forces in the battle as a whole. The divisional artillery was divided into a headquarters howitzer battalion, a target-acquisition battery, three forward assault battalions, and one general support battalion. The forward assault battalions each controlled 24 M109 self-propelled 155-mm (6·1-in) howitzers, and each battalion routinely supported one of the division's brigades. The M109 is fully tracked and offers a high level of battlefield mobility and protection, so the battalion could be divided into two sections capable in independent operations. The general support battalion was equipped with 12 M110 self-propelled 8-in (203-mm) howitzers and nine extremely capable Multiple Launch Rocket Systems. The latter is a new type based on a fully tracked chassis and carries a training and elevating 12-tube launcher for no fewer than 12 long-range rockets, each of 8·94-in (227-mm) caliber. These rockets are accurate and versatile carriers for payloads that can range from a single large warhead via 28 parachute-retarded antitank mines to 644 free-fall antitank/antipersonnel bomblets.

The divisional artillery of the so-called Division '86 developed for the "AirLand Battle 2000" concept had a greater number of weapons than earlier divisions, but its real superiority lay in the greater responsiveness and flexibility of its organization. This provided much-enhanced battlefield power when matched with other improvements such as greater ammunition resupply capability, faster and more accurate fire direction, and the integration of automated systems.

A More Powerful U.S. Navy

As a continental land mass separated from Europe by the Atlantic Ocean and from the Far East by the Pacific Ocean, the United States needs a large and powerful navy able to operate effectively on both of these oceans simultaneously, and as well as in other areas. Thus the twin tasks undertaken by the U.S. Navy are power projection and sea control.

The concept of power projection involves the deployment of American military strength and associated political influence to areas of the globe distant from the United States, while sea control involves gaining and maintaining mastery over the maritime communications between the United States and those distant areas. Thus, power projection and sea control are interrelated, for power projection is impossible without sea control, and sea control is pointless without power projection as a goal. The navy must therefore be able to control the seas that American forces have to cross in order to reach their objectives; it must also dominate the air over the operating area so that air and amphibious operations can be undertaken effectively. At the same time, sea control is facilitated by the presence of power-projection forces at the far end of the protected route, for this presence both keeps the enemy on the defensive and provides a springboard from which the far end of the route can be protected.

To this extent, therefore, power projection and sea control are both aspects of the same problem. The difficulty lies in balancing the forces needed for "offensive" power projection and "defensive" sea control.

In time of war, of course, the problem largely disappears because the financial and physical resources to address the problem become virtually unlimited. The United States has the capability to build virtually every ship and all aircraft that its navy might need. It may take time, but it does not affect the fact that the problem can be largely ignored by longer-term

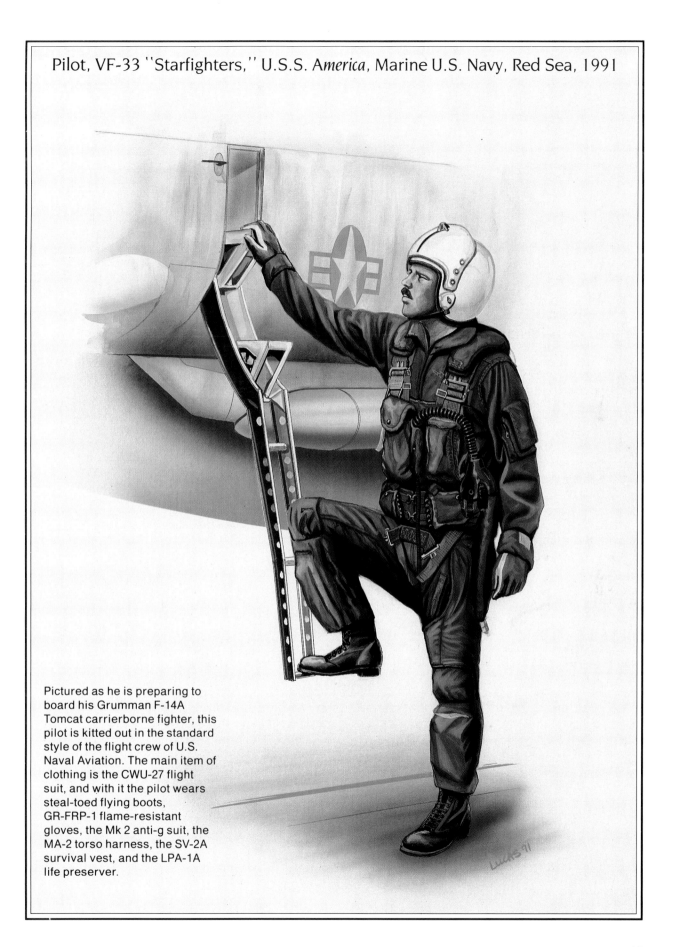

Pilot, VF-33 "Starfighters," U.S.S. *America*, Marine U.S. Navy, Red Sea, 1991

Pictured as he is preparing to board his Grumman F-14A Tomcat carrierborne fighter, this pilot is kitted out in the standard style of the flight crew of U.S. Naval Aviation. The main item of clothing is the CWU-27 flight suit, and with it the pilot wears steal-toed flying boots, GR-FRP-1 flame-resistant gloves, the Mk 2 anti-g suit, the MA-2 torso harness, the SV-2A survival vest, and the LPA-1A life preserver.

The latest type of aircraft carrier to enter U.S. Navy service is the nuclear-powered ''Nimitz'' class, eventually to total eight ships and represented here by the lead ship, the U.S.S. *Nimitz*, which was commissioned in May 1975. Each ship has a full-load displacement in the order of 91,485 tons and is powered by two pressurized, water-cooled reactors supplying steam to four sets of geared turbines that deliver 260,000 horsepower to four shafts for a speed of more than 30 knots, but basically unlimited range. The ship's complement is 155 officers and 2,980 crew excluding the air group, which has 365 officers and 2,435 personnel for the operation of some 90 aircraft. The ship carries ''aviation consumables'' (fuel and weapons) for 16 days of sustained operations without replenishment and has the standard fit of four steam catapults and four deck-edge lifts.

planners. In time of peace, however, the problem is very real, for planners have to take into account limited budgets and, to a lesser extent, reduced personnel. More of one type of vessel inevitably means fewer of another type, and the staffing of a large warship inevitably means fewer crew for the smaller vessels. This naturally leads to factional infighting as the leaders of particular service branches seek to preserve their own branch. It is very rare, for example, that a naval aviator would agree that greater submarine construction was needed if this meant a curtailment of naval aviation.

A Viable Navy?

In the period immediately after World War II, the U.S. Navy was faced with coming to terms with the atomic bomb, whose availability threw traditional naval thinking into complete confusion. Indeed, there were many naval thinkers who suggested that the atomic bomb rendered conventional forces completely superfluous, since a single weapon could destroy a complete task force.

The arguments about the viability of naval forces was still raging when the Korean War broke out in 1950. Operations in this conflict suggested firmly that naval forces still had a valued part to play in modern warfare. The war showed conclusively that the two main elements on which the navy should be built were the aircraft carrier and the amphibious warfare vessel, at the center of specialized

task forces. After the end of the Korean War in 1953, there was a massive program of new construction including, in the period between 1955 and 1962, the commissioning of seven large carriers including one nuclear-powered ship.

Carrierborne Strategic Aircraft

These carriers were designed to operate not only conventional attack aircraft such as the piston-engined Douglas AD (later A-1) Skyraider and the jet-powered Douglas A4D (later A-4) Skyhawk, but also nuclear-armed strategic strike aircraft, such as the highly impressive Douglas A3D (later A-3) Skywarrior, which could devastate targets deep in the U.S.S.R. from launch points in many parts of the surrounding international waters.

A large construction program was also devoted to amphibious warfare vessels of various types. At the same time, large numbers of cruisers and destroyers built in World War II were retained and extensively upgraded for the twin tasks of escorting carrier task forces and providing gunfire support for amphibious warfare task forces.

Advent of the Surface-to-air Missile

Throughout the 1950s, the guided missile emerged as an increasingly powerful and reliable weapon. Unlike its communist

Huge numbers of Kuwaiti refugees fled to Jordan to avoid the Iraqi military.

potential enemy, the Soviet navy, the U.S. Navy had large numbers of carriers with substantial and effective complements of attack and strike aircraft. It saw little value in surface-to-surface missiles launched from submarines or ships and devoted little of its budget or tactical thinking to this weapon. The surface-to-air missile, on the other hand, found a ready home in American naval thinking. It was one of the cornerstones on which the defense of carrier task forces could be built. During the 1950s, therefore, the navy devoted a very large part of its budget to the development and deployment of a family of related surface-to-air missiles. These weapons were the long-range Talos with rocket and ramjet propulsion, the medium-range Terrier with rocket propulsion, and the short-range Tartar, also with rocket propulsion.

By the first part of the 1960s, these weapons had been installed on a number of U.S. warships, starting with converted war-time heavy and light cruisers, and then proceeding to three 10-ship classes of Terrier-armed "frigates" that soon became cruisers, and finally a single but very large class of Tartar-equipped destroyers. The navy also launched a program to develop the Typhoon as a very long-range successor to the Talos with a similar hybrid propulsion arrangement, but it was cancelled in 1963. (The concept was revived later as the Aegis system, using

the Standard Missile that is the ultimate development of the concept embodied in the Terrier and Tartar missiles.)

During the 1950s, the Soviets also started a huge program of development designed to turn the Soviet navy into a true blue-water force capable of meeting the U.S. Navy on terms of equity, but the program could yield significant results only in the longer term. Despite its considerable growth during the 1950s, the Soviet navy remained a coast-defense force that offered no threat to the sea control of the U.S. Navy. Indeed, so limited was the threat of the Soviet navy that the only sea-control ships built by the U.S. Navy in this period were a comparatively small number of diesel-powered destroyer escorts that had little real advance over the destroyer escorts built in World War II.

Shortage of Antisubmarine Capability

The one exception to the Soviets' inability to threaten American sea control was in the eastern Atlantic, where an emerging threat was detected from the fleet of steadily improving Soviet submarines based in the Kola peninsula on the extreme northwestern corner of the U.S.S.R. Even so, the only counter to this threat was from "Essex" class carriers built during World War II and converted into antisubmarine ships carrying Grumman S2F (later S-2) Tracker fixed-wing aircraft and Sikorsky HSS-1 (later SH-34) Seabat helicopters. Each converted carrier became the core of a specialized submarine hunter/killer group that was also used for convoy escort. The main task of defeating Soviet submarines in the eastern Atlantic was undertaken by the navies of the United States' European partners in the North Atlantic Treaty Organization, which received considerable Mutual Defense Aid Program funding for the development of their antisubmarine forces.

Submarine-launched Missiles

From 1960 onward, the navy's role in American nuclear capability against the U.S.S.R. was steadily switched from the strike aircraft of the supercarriers to nuclear-powered submarines, each carrying 16 underwater-launched Polaris ballistic missiles. Some thought that the switch heralded the end of the road for the usefulness of the carrier, but they were soon disabused of the notion by events in the Vietnam War. For nearly 10 years up to 1972, the U.S. Navy was heavily involved in a twofold program of attacks against targets in North Vietnam and support for the allied forces in South Vietnam. Over the same period, studies were undertaken for new types of nuclear-powered warships (aircraft carriers and their missile-armed cruiser escorts), and construction was started on 60 amphibious warfare vessels to replace the increasingly obsolescent force of vessels built in World War II.

Rehabilitation of Old Ships instead of New Construction

The emphasis had been placed squarely on ships for the navy's power-projection role. These ships were extremely capable, but they were also extremely costly, and their construction meant that the navy's sea-control forces were neglected. Admittedly, during the early 1960s, many of the surviving destroyers of World War II underwent the FRAM (Fleet Rehabilitation And Modernization) refits that saw the introduction of more modern antisubmarine capability (new sonars, ASROC antisubmarine rockets that dropped lightweight homing torpedoes into the sea near the target submarine, and DASH drone antisubmarine helicopters).

From the early 1960s, however, a small number of destroyer escorts (later frigates) were built, beginning with the two "Bronstein" class units. These ships were designed to break away from the high costs of current fleet escorts, but still provide a good level of capability against the latest Soviet nuclear-powered submarines, which were considerably faster and quieter than their predecessors. The new frigates were dedicated antisubmarine vessels of limited performance and poor maneuverability, but they had a very advanced combination of massive bow sonar together with ASROC and DASH antisubmarine weapons. The concept was developed from the experimental "Bronstein" class into the 10-strong "Garcia" class, but the following "Brooke" class added a surface-to-air missile capability in a move that increased costs so considerably that construction was halted after just six ships.

The Threat of "Block Obsolescence"

By the middle 1960s, the U.S. Navy was finally faced with the realization that the war-built escorts on which it had relied for some 20 years were approaching the stage of "block obsolescence." The result was the huge "Knox" class of 46 dedicated antisubmarine frigates that entered service between 1969 and 1974. The emphasis was placed on a very high antisubmarine capability but low cost, so while the electronics, weapons, and basic single-shaft design were modeled on those of the "Brooke" and "Garcia" classes, the hull was enlarged to allow the use of non-pressure-fired boilers. The type has proved generally successful in service, but considerable criticism was raised about the ship's poor performance and agility. Its lack of antiship armament also caused concern, but has been remedied by the modifi-

Captain, AH-64A Apache Pilot, 101st Airborne Division (Air Assault), U.S. Army, Saudi Arabia, 1991

This officer is typical of the pilots allocated to the aviation brigade of this air-assault formation, but carries the $15,000 helmet associated with the IHADSS (Integrated Helmet And Display Sighting System) that forms one of the most important operational features of the McDonnell Douglas Helicopters AH-64A Apache battlefield helicopter. Other elements of the captain's kit are the CWU-27 flying suit and the SRU-21 survival vest. The latter has an attached leather holster for a Smith & Wesson Model 10 revolver, and its pockets are designed to hold the URC-68 survival radio, flares, strobe lights, compass, and other survival items.

cation of the ASROC launcher to carry eight Harpoon antiship missiles instead of the same numbers of ASROCs.

This criticism led to the so-called DDX design that finally matured in the "Spruance" class whose 31 ships were commissioned between 1975 and 1983. They are more capable and highly sophisticated ships, offering antiaircraft, antiship, and antisubmarine capabilities, but only at a displacement three times greater than that of the ships they replaced, and at very high cost.

By 1970, the only new classes under serious consideration were once more power-projection types such as the "Nimitz" class of nuclear-powered attack carriers, the "Tarawa" class of amphibious assault ships, the "Virginia" class of nuclear-powered missile cruisers, the "Spruance" class of missile destroyers, and the "Los Angeles" class of nuclear-powered fleet submarines. Of these, the last three were designed for the fleet role in support of the type of carrier battle groups that had replaced carrier task forces.

Admiral Zumwalt and Project 60

This situation had developed under three Chiefs of Naval Operations. All were naval aviators and were thus inclined to the power-projection concept. In 1970, however, Admiral Elmo Zumwalt became Chief of Naval Operations. His background as a surface ship officer convinced him that the demands of the Vietnam War had led to the navy's becoming badly unbalanced. Zumwalt was sure that the navy's sea-control capability had declined to a critical level, especially as the Soviets' long-term development was beginning to offer a challenge to American naval superiority. Zumwalt highlighted the threat to allied convoys in the Atlantic during any war between the Warsaw Pact and NATO, and rightly emphasized the fact that the converted "Essex" class carriers and sea-control destroyers were on average more than 25 years old. Even with the "Spruance" class of multirole destroyers, the navy had only 180 of the 250 escorts it had fixed as the minimum for completion of its assigned tasks.

The inevitable conclusion was that the navy needed large numbers of new ships, and it needed them quickly. Zumwalt's solution was his "high/low" combination. The high end of the spectrum would be covered by high-capability ships to undertake the power-projection role in high-threat areas, while the low end would be the responsibility of modest-performance ships that would cost comparatively little and could therefore be built in large numbers for the sea-control role.

Within 60 days of taking office, Zumwalt had introduced his Project 60 as the blueprint for naval construction in the 1970s. Zumwalt recognized that the high end of his concept was already underway in the development and construction program begun during 1970, and his only alteration was the cancellation of the last four of the planned nine "Tarawa" class. Zumwalt balanced the high end of the spectrum with a new low end financed largely by the retirement of elderly ships. The low end of the spectrum was provided by four new classes, of which the most important were the so-called Patrol Frigate and the Sea Control Ship.

The PF became the 51-strong "Oliver Hazard Perry" class of missile frigates. The type was basically a development of the frigates built in the 1960s, but had two gas turbines powering two shafts for adequate speed and good maneuverability. Revised electronics and armament give antiaircraft and antiship capabilities a priority nearly as high as the antisubmarine capability. The ships of this large and important class were commissioned between 1981 and 1989.

The SCS was a limited-capability carrier without an angled flight deck. It was designed to operate 14 Sikorsky SH-3 Sea King antisubmarine helicopters, as well as three British Aerospace AV-8A Harrier aircraft that have the ability to make short take-offs and vertical landings. The SCS was planned as replacement for the "Essex" class carriers, and its low price tag meant that eight cost the same as one "Nimitz" class carrier.

Other Project 60 aspects were the development of the Kaman SH-2 Seasprite manned light helicopter as the Light Airborne Multi-Purpose System to replace the DASH drone; the development of the Harpoon missile so that powerful antiship capability could be spread throughout the fleet; and the development of a network of satellite-based intelligence and communications systems to coordinate the activities of what were now becoming sensor and weapon platforms instead of just plain warships.

Zumwalt retired in 1974, and the battle between power-projection and sea-control advocates picked up once more.

Death of the Sea-Control Ship

The initial victim of the struggle was the SCS. Trials were held in which the "Tarawa" class U.S.S. *Saipan* played the part of the SCS. In the evaluation of these trials, the SCS was declared highly vulnerable to the threat posed by the Soviets' long-range bombers and missile launchers. The SCS was therefore cancelled, though the real reason was clearly the concern of naval aviators that funding of the SCS would inevitably result in slashed budgets for the attack carriers and high-performance aircraft in which they believed. Another aspect of the naval aviators' concern was Zumwalt's suggestion that during peace and in the early stages of war, the semi-expendable SCSs should be deployed in high-risk areas, to be replaced later by the more capable attack carriers. The naval aviators felt that any implementation of such a policy would so erode the credibility of the large attack carriers that funding would be cut by Congress.

The naval aviators did have to make one concession, however. From 1975, the dedicated attack carrier became the multimission carrier. Some of its attack/strike aircraft were replaced by two antisubmarine squadrons (one of Lockheed S-3A Viking fixed-wing aircraft and the other of Sikorsky SH-3H Sea King helicopters). This change enhanced the ability of such carriers to provide effective long-range cover for convoys and to undertake general submarine hunting in conjunction with the SOSUS seabed surveillance system. Just as importantly, it gave carrier battle groups the capability to protect themselves at long range against Soviet submarines armed with antiship cruise missiles. By the end of the 1970s, many of the U.S. Navy's warships were fitted with the Harpoon, a comparatively light but effective medium-range antiship missile. Also in the offing was the Tomahawk cruise missile, a somewhat larger missile that offered capabilities equal to the best cruise missiles deployed by the Soviets. The imminent arrival of the Tomahawk and its very long range again raised tensions between the naval aviators and advocates of the surface ship. To secure the highest possible accuracy over long range, the Tomahawk can benefit from a very costly satellite-based Extended Horizon Command and Control System or mid-course guidance update from vertical take-off aircraft scattered among a comparatively large number of surface ships. The naval aviators saw these possibilities as threatening the supremacy of their carriers, and they objected to the scattering of STOVL aircraft on large numbers of ships as uneconomical in terms of space and maintenance facilities.

Naval aviators have, with some justification, constantly stressed the supremacy of the aircraft carrier as a versatile and cost-effective warship. They maintain that any shift of emphasis from the aircraft carrier would mean the adoption of an essentially defensive sea-control system that would play into the tactical hands of the modern Soviet navy.

Increased Spending in the Reagan Era

When Ronald Reagan was inaugurated as president during January 1981, the related financial and political situations began to change in the navy's favor. Reagan was firmly committed to the concept of reaching accord with the Soviets from a position of military and diplomatic strength, a somewhat different approach from that of his predecessor, who seemed bent on reaching accommodation with the Soviets through simple mediation.

President Reagan thus created the political and financial situation in which the navy could flourish. The provision of funds would allow its growth from a 450- to a 600-ship fleet that would include new super-carriers and their escorts, as well as large numbers of sea-control ships and Tomahawk missiles. Considerable strides toward this goal were made in continued construction of the "Ohio" class of ballistic missile submarines, "Los Angeles" class of fleet submarines, "Ticonderoga" class of missile cruisers, "Arleigh Birke" class of missile destroyers, and new amphibious warfare vessels, plus the reactivation of four "Iowa" class battleships as missile-armed command ships with an extremely powerful gun bombardment capability. As the Reagan administration continued, however, it became clear that the U.S. economy could not sustain the huge demand of this and other military programs, and under President George Bush, various schemes have been eliminated and the overall plans cut back to more realistic levels.

The Power of the Air Force

When the U.S. Army Air Forces were turned into the U.S. Air Force by the National Security Act on September 18, 1947, they were organized into five major commands. Two were legacies of World War II, namely the U.S. Air Forces in Europe (formerly the U.S. Strategic Air Forces in Europe), and the Far East Air Force, which soon became the Pacific Air Forces (formerly the U.S. Strategic Air Forces in the Far East). On March 21, 1946, these two commands had been joined by three new commands based in the continental United States, namely the Strategic Air Command, Tactical Air Command, and Air Defense Command.

By the end of 1970, the number of major commands in the air force had grown to 15. Two of these (the Strategic Air Command and Tactical Air Command) were concerned primarily with maintaining the United States' deterrent capability with nuclear and conventional weapons. Another five (Air Defense Command, U.S. Air Forces in Europe, Pacific Air Forces, Southern Command, and Alaskan Air Command) also contributed to the policy of deterrence by providing a high level of defensive capability. An additional five (Military Airlift Command, Air Training Command, Headquarters Command, Systems Command, and the Air University) operated in the support role, and the air force's basic structure was completed by Logistics Command, Communications Service, and Security Service.

Command Strengths in 1971

By 1971, the basic strengths and roles of the various commands were as follows. The Strategic Air Command, the air force's main deterrent arm, included the 2nd, 8th, and 15th Air Forces (plus additional aircraft and missile divisions)

Much of the survivability of American warplanes in the face of sophisticated air-defense systems is provided by electronic countermeasures (ECM) designed to jam or mislead enemy radar used to lock onto targets and guide missiles. Although most of the latest warplanes carry a mixture of internal and external ECM systems, most of the older types carry just external pods, such as this ALQ-119 jammer seen under the wing of a Fairchild Republic A-10A Thunderbolt II antitank and battlefield close-support warplane.

with about 450 jet bombers and more than 1,000 intercontinental ballistic missiles. Tactical Air Command was the air force's main operator of tactical air power and was particularly geared for mobile operations using large numbers of tactical transport aircraft; the command's organization included the 9th, 12th, and 19th Air Forces with a wide-ranging assortment of tactical fighter, reconnaissance, inflight refueling, and troop carrier wings. Aerospace Defense Command was responsible for the air defense of the continental United States and was fully integrated with the American-Canadian NORAD (North American Air Defence Command) organization; Aerospace Defense Command's six air divisions included manned interceptors, airborne early warning aircraft, and surface-to-air missiles. The U.S. Air Forces in Europe command was part of the American contribution to the NATO defense of Europe, and its area of responsibility stretched in a vast arc from northern Norway to Pakistan; the

command included the 3rd, 16th, and 17th Air Forces, with a miscellany of aircraft for tactical, logistical, and rescue roles. The Pacific Air Forces command in the Pacific basin fulfilled a role comparable with that of USAFE (though not, of course, under the NATO banner); the command was made up of the 5th, 7th, and 13th Air Forces, as well as a number of air divisions and other units attached for operations in Vietnam. Alaskan Air Command was responsible for the air defense of Alaska and operated the radar sites of the Distant Early Warning network. Military Airlift Command was responsible for logistic airlift support of all three U.S. services on a worldwide basis, using heavy transport aircraft operated from bases in the eastern U.S.A. by the 21st Air Force and in the western U.S.A. by the 22nd Air Force; the MAC also controlled the Aerospace Rescue and Recovery Service, the Air Weather Service, the Cartographic and Geodetic Service, and other specialized units. The Air Force Reserve had been created in August 1968 as a separate operating agency as a successor to the Continental Air Command; the AFRES provided a large part of the air force's transport and rescue capability through its 32 airlift groups, four tactical air support groups, two special operations groups, and five aerospace rescue and recovery squadrons. The Air National Guard was part of the Air Force Reserve Forces, providing an aircraft and personnel reserve ready for despatch at a moment's notice to reinforce active forces: ANG squadrons flew tactical fighters, reconnaissance aircraft, transports, and airborne early warning aircraft.

A New Generation of Aircraft

The Vietnam War had a major impact on the approach of the air force to tactics and aircraft. The most notable change was a move away from complex and scarcely maintainable warplanes that could easily reach Mach 2, but were lacking in maneuverability. Their place was taken by lighter and considerably more maintainable tactical aircraft. They lacked their predecessor's outright performance, but were considerable more agile and able to undertake at least two main tasks with considerable capability. Tactical types that had entered service in the Vietnam War, such as the General Dynamics F-111 "swing-wing" long-range interdictor and the Vought A-7 medium attack plane, remained in service and development, but a new feel was brought to the air force by the adoption of more advanced tactical warplanes such as the McDonnell Douglas F-15 Eagle air superiority fighter and the General Dynamics F-16 Fighting Falcon air combat fighter.

So far as tactics were concerned, the air force at last realized the fallacy of planning and training only for war in a European environment against Soviet-dominated Warsaw Pact forces. It revised its thinking to cover a whole range of tactical air operations against any possible enemy in any part of the world.

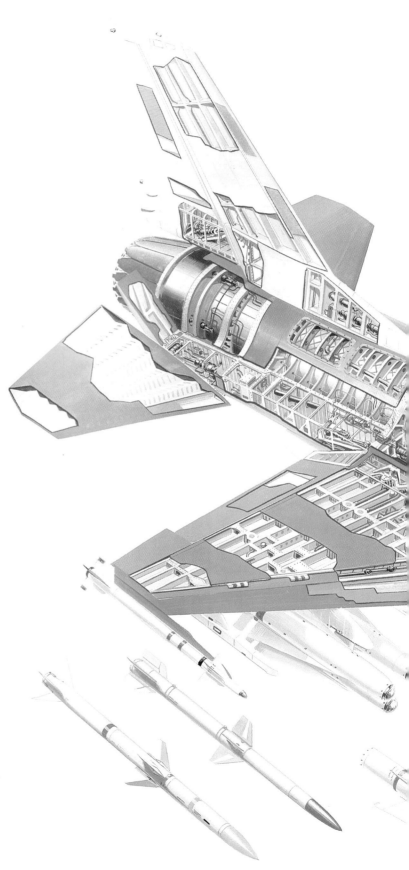

One of the finest warplanes available to the U.S. Air Force for the war with Iraq was the General Dynamics F-16C Fighting Falcon, the latest version of a type designed as an air combat fighter, but steadily developed as a wholly exceptional multirole fighter. The type has a blended fuselage/wing design and is basically unstable. It is controlled with the aid of a "fly-by-wire" computer system that translates the pilot's control inputs into movement of the right control surfaces to exactly the required degree. This ability gives the craft superb agility, and the pilot can absorb the forces imposed on his body as he or she sits in a semi-reclining position under a canopy that provides all-round fields of vision. This cutaway diagram of the Fighting Falcon reveals the type's structure, the arrangement of the major features, and a selection of the stores that can be carried externally. These include free-fall and "Snakeye" retarded bombs, rocket-launcher pods, cannon pods, air-to-air and air-to-surface missiles, guided bombs, and electronic countermeasures pods. Located in the port wing/fuselage chine is the 20-mm M61A1 Vulcan 20-mm cannon, and on the starboard side of the air inlet is the LANTIRN targeting pod (matched on the port side by the navigation pod). The weapons shown on the wings are two AIM-9 Sidewinder air-to-air missiles at the tips and two triplets of AGM-65 Maverick air-to-surface missiles under the wings.

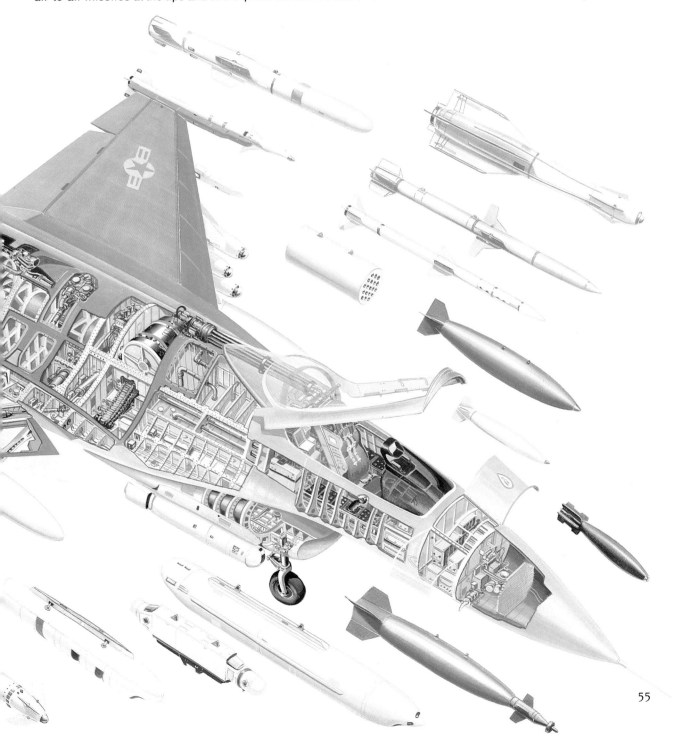

Strength in the Mid-1980s

By the mid-1980s, the U.S. Air Force had some 7,300 aircraft on strength, with a further 485 and 460 in the hands of the Air Force Reserve and Air National Guard respectively. The service operated from 94 bases in the continental United States and 43 main bases in friendly countries. The Air Force Reserve and Air National Guard operated from 85 American bases, some of them shared with the air force. At these bases, most fighter and attack squadrons operated between 18 and 24 aircraft each. Bomber squadrons had between 12 and 19 aircraft each, except in the case of FB-111 units, which had 12 or 13 aircraft each. Transport squadrons varied in size according to their equipment, from 16 aircraft in units with the Lockheed C-130 Hercules, 17 aircraft in units operating the Lockheed C-5A Galaxy, to 18 aircraft in units operating the Lockheed C-141 StarLifter. Squadrons operating specialized high-technology aircraft such as the Boeing E-3 Sentry airborne warning and control system aircraft could differ in size between two and 17 aircraft.

At this time, the air force had a strength of 599,000 service and 243,000 civilian personnel, and its technical inventory included 363 strategic bombers, 1,052 intercontinental ballistic missiles, 3,026 fighter and attack aircraft, 392 reconnaissance and electronic warfare aircraft, 544 inflight refueling tanker aircraft, 828 transport aircraft, 238 helicopters, 250 utility, observation, and search-and-rescue aircraft, and 1,664 trainers. Within this total, Strategic Air Command operated 316 Boeing B-52 Stratofortress heavy bombers (75 B-52Ds, 151 G-52Gs and 90 B-52Hs) and 63 General Dynamics FB-111A medium bombers, 1,000 Boeing LGM-30 Minuteman (400 Minuteman II and 600 Minuteman III), and 52 Martin Marietta LGM-25 Titan II intercontinental ballistic missiles, 51 reconnaissance aircraft (16 Boeing RC-135s, nine Lockheed SR-71 "Blackbirds," eight Lockheed U-2Rs, and 18 Lockheed TR-1s), 27 aerial commands posts (21 Boeing EC-135s and six Boeing E-4Bs), and 646 Boeing KC-135A Stratotanker inflight refueling tankers with 60 McDonnell Douglas KC-10A Extender dual-role tanker/transport aircraft in the pipeline.

One of the more recent exercises adopted as a regular feature of the U.S. forces' training schedule is "Bright Star," practicing a deployment to Egypt. Here Lockheed C-130 Hercules transports of the U.S. Air Force's Tactical Air Command are seen on an Egyptian airfield in the unusual company of a Soviet-built bomber, a Tupolev Tu-16 "Badger," of the Egyptian air force.

Upgraded versions of current aircraft were developed and introduced whenever possible, and a continuous program of research and development meant that the air force was provided with "state of the art" aircraft and equipment as soon as it was technically possible. The training regime was revised radically once the lessons of the Vietnam War had been digested, and by the late 1980s, the air force was in very good shape, both technically and tactically.

During the 1980s the United States had been involved in several small "brushfire" wars that revealed technical and tactical matters that needed improvement, and these problems had generally been corrected by the end of the decade. This was just as well, for the country was about to become involved in its largest conflict since the end of the Vietnam War. It became the leading light of an allied force assembled under the banner of the United Nations to wrest back Kuwait from Iraqi control.

Crisis in the Persian Gulf

When the Iraqi war with Iran ended in an armistice resulting from the stalemate on the battlefield, Iraq as a nation was proud of its effort against its much larger neighbor. However, the Iraqi nation generally ignored the fact that Iraq had started this unprovoked war. Though most Iraqis were heartily glad that peace had returned, they also knew that the country had been effectively bankrupted. The war had resulted in the loss of huge oil exports, and vast quantities of foreign money had been borrowed to buy the advanced weapons with which the Iraqi forces had hoped to defeat their considerably more numerous enemy.

With the return of peace, Iraq's creditors started to exert pressure to get their loans repaid. This was difficult, for under the leadership of President Saddam Hussein, Iraq not only needed to rebuild is shattered economy, but it also wanted to expand its already considerable forces and equip them with more up-to-date weaponry. This meant borrowing even more money instead of the repayment of existing loans, and the only way in which Iraq could hope to meet both requirements was to generate large quantities of additional finance.

The most obvious solution for Iraq was to put pressure on Kuwait. A long-standing dispute existed about the ownership of a major oilfield straddling the frontier between the two countries, in the region just south of the Iraqi town of Safwan. Saddam Hussein felt that Kuwait lacked the political and military strength to withstand a campaign of sustained Iraqi pressure and gambled on divisions among the nations of the Western world to prevent any effective support for Kuwait.

Iraq Sets Its Sights on Kuwait's Wealth

The campaign to secure Kuwait's wealth for Iraq effectively began on July 17, 1990, when Saddam Hussein accused the oil-producing states of the Persian Gulf of conspiring with the United States to cut the price of crude oil, thereby "stabbing Iraq in the back with a poisoned dagger." The Iraqi president then added that "Iraqis will not forget that cutting necks is better than cutting the means of living." The pace of the emerging confrontation increased on the following day when the Iraqi foreign minister, Tariq Aziz, told a meeting of the Arab League that Kuwait had built military positions on Iraqi soil and, adding a financial burden to this affront against Iraqi sovereignty, had also stolen more than $2 billion worth of Iraqi oil by drilling slantwise bores from the Kuwaiti side of the border into the Iraqi half of the disputed oilfield. One day later, an Iraqi newspaper thunderously concluded that "We have been too patient with the violations by Kuwait."

In three days, Iraq had set the international scene for its planned aggression against Kuwait and begun the process of gearing its people into a mood to support the invasion that was soon to follow.

The Middle East has long been a region in which words are sometimes far stronger than the actions which follow. On July 22 President Mubarak of Egypt

President George Bush displayed an excellent combination of political common sense and personal determination in the crisis with Iraq.

troops and further quantities of armor massed in the frontier region. Despite pleas to the contrary, the Iraqi delegation was not prepared to negotiate in any meaningful way, but just repeated its demands for Kuwaiti "compensation." On August 1 it was clear that the talks had no chance of resolving the increasingly dangerous situation.

Iraq Invades and Occupies Kuwait

Yet the apparent willingness of the Iraqis to talk had bought Saddam Hussein the time to complete his preparations, and at 2:00 a.m. on August 2 Iraqi forces swept forward into Kuwait. As the first news of the Iraqi invasion spread to a world that had not really believed that Iraq could undertake so blatant a piece of aggression, Iraq warned that "We will turn Kuwait into a graveyard if anyone tries to commit aggression."

The frontier was held on the Kuwaiti side by only light forces with no heavy weapons or supporting armor. The rumble of Iraqi tanks was followed by an unopposed barrage of high-velocity shells fired at very short range as the invasion forces crossed the frontier. The Kuwaitis responded as best they could with small arms and automatic weapons, but could offer no more than a token resistance before falling back or being overrun. The Iraqi advance plunged into Kuwait in five main columns designed to converge on Kuwait City. The advance was later described by an American officer as a "cakewalk" for the Iraqis, who had total supremacy on the ground and in the air. Air superiority and close support capability was provided by large numbers of French-supplied Dassault-Breguet Mirage F1 and Soviet-supplied Mikoyan-Gurevich fighters of various types. The Kuwaiti Air Force had only 54 fixed- and rotary-wing combat aircraft. In the face of the overwhelming superiority brought to bear against it, it offered only scant resistance before sending most of its surviving aircraft south to safety in Saudi Arabia. There was only one known Kuwaiti victory in the invasion period, the shooting down of an Iraqi helicopter before the Kuwaiti pilot was forced to

said, "The dispute between Iraq, Kuwait, and the United Arab Emirates is a cloud which will soon pass." Yet, just two days later, on July 24, Iraq moved some 30,000 men and substantial armored forces up to its frontier with Kuwait, followed one day later by a demand that Kuwait pay Iraq compensation of $2 billion for the oil it had "stolen." Saddam Hussein nonetheless assured President Mubarak that despite these military moves, Iraq would not attack Kuwait. This seems to have reassured the Arab world, and on July 26 the Arab Times of Kuwait told its readers that "It's over!" The situation was very far from easing, however, and the Organization of Petroleum Exporting Countries raised the price of crude oil to $21 per barrel, thereby yielding to Iraqi pressure designed to boost the value of its oil exports, the country's only major generator of hard currency.

On July 31, Kuwait and Iraqi officials gathered in neutral territory, the Saudi Arabian city of Jeddah, to discuss their border problem, while 100,000 Iraqi

break away by the devastating quantities of light antiaircraft fire that the Iraqi ground forces poured into the sky.

Warned by telephone of the Iraqi thrusts converging on the city, the Emir of Kuwait and the members of the ruling al-Sabah family who were in the country left about 5:00 a.m. and so escaped the attentions of the elite Iraqi Republican Guard units sent to capture them.

Within the Kuwaiti defense establishment, there was great confusion, for although Kuwaiti officers who had visited Iraq in the last few weeks had warned of the invasion's imminence, their reports had gone unheeded. Even after the Iraqi invasion had begun, no one at the Kuwaiti defense department had taken it upon himself to declare a state of mobilization, so the few Kuwaiti units that offered resistance to the invaders did so as a result of their own initiatives. The defense was at best sporadic, but in any case, it could not have checked the Iraqi advance for long.

With total inevitability, Iraq claimed that it had been invited into Kuwait, but this claim was soon proved untrue by Kuwaiti calls for international assistance and by the establishment in Saudi Arabia of a "Free Provisional Kuwaiti Government."

International Opposition Gathers Strength

At an emergency meeting of the United Nations' Security Council, the Iraqi invasion was condemned. Already, international moves were underway. The United States, United Kingdom, and France froze Iraqi and Kuwaiti assets in their countries and banned all trade with Iraq. The U.S.S.R. halted all deliveries of arms to Iraq. The United States also put the military machine in motion by sending the carrier U.S.S. *Independence* from the Indian Ocean toward the Persian Gulf.

On August 3, the United States announced the creation of a naval task force for possible operations in the Persian Gulf. After the Arab League had condemned the Iraqi aggression against Kuwait, the U.S. urged both Saudi Arabia and Turkey to close the pipelines through which Iraqi oil flowed to non-Iraqi ports. Throughout the day, Iraqi forces continued to consolidate their grip on Kuwait, moving troops south into the region adjoining Saudi Arabia. Despite the continued forward movement of its troops, Iraq announced that it would pull all of its troops out of Kuwait on August 5.

Even though Iraq categorically denied on August 4 that it had any hostile intent toward Saudi Arabia, during that day Iraqi forces entered both of the neutral zones separating Kuwait from Saudi Arabia, and the state of tension therefore continued to increase. On August 5, there was no sign that the Iraqis were about to pull back their forces as they had promised two days earlier, and President Bush reported that the Iraqis had "lied once again." On the same day, the European Community decided to freeze all Kuwaiti assets in its member countries and to start an immediate boycott of Iraqi oil. Saddam Hussein responded to this major move by warning all countries with nationals in Kuwait not even to consider the possibility of sanctions against Iraq.

Embargo on Trade with Iraq

On August 6, the Security Council met once more to tackle the Kuwaiti question and, with Cuba and North Yemen abstaining, voted to place an embargo on trade of any type with Iraq. Saddam Hussein's response was the claim that any embargo would merely delay the Iraqi withdrawal from Kuwait. At the same time, Iraqi forces began to round up American, British, and German nationals in Kuwait.

American Forces on the Move

Throughout this period, events continued to move with considerable speed as the crisis deepened steadily. On August 7, President Bush ordered the despatch to Saudi Arabia of 4,000 men of the 82nd Airborne Division and numbers of F-15 fighters, and announced the intention of the United States to participate in the enforcement of the UN embargo. On the same day, Saddam Hussein said that the

Baghdad
For further
references see
pages
66, 77, 78, 82

Men of the 24th
Infantry Division
(Mechanized) move
out to the aircraft that
will transport them to
Saudi Arabia in
Operation ''Desert
Shield.''

''Croesus of Kuwait'' had been over-thrown, thereby trying to win support from Arab groups unhappy with the immense economic and political power of the families ruling the Gulf states. The effort had virtually no useful effect, for it failed to take into account the fact that the oil wealth which had turned the ruling families into Croesuses had also brought about an enormous improve-ment in the living standards of most Arabs of the Gulf region.

On August 8, President Bush an-nounced that the American mission in the Gulf was ''wholly defensive...A line has been drawn in the sand.'' On the same day, Saddam Hussein announced the annexation of Kuwait as the 19th province of Iraq, thereby ending all speculation about an Iraqi withdrawal and putting the lie to the Iraqi president's earlier claims. A day later the Security Council ruled that the annexation was illegal. Saddam Hussein, disregarding this United Nations' decision, ordered all foreign embassies in Kuwait to close their doors and shift their operations to

Baghdad by August 24. On the same day, Iraq closed all its borders for ''security reasons,'' and the United Kingdom sent two air squadrons to Saudi Arabia.

The extent to which Saddam Hussein had miscalculated the feeling of the Arab world became clearer on August 10, when 12 out of an invited 20 Arab heads of state met in Cairo at the invitation of President Mubarak. Despite the unhappiness of some leaders, it was decided that a pan-Arab force should be raised and despatched to Saudi Arabia. On the same day, the countries of the European Community decided to defy Saddam Hussein's order and keep their embassies in Kuwait open for as long as possible.

A Change in Iraqi Emphasis

Saddam Hussein now changed propaganda tack to try to win Arab allies. Realizing that his effort to create and use envy of the ruling families' wealth had failed, the Iraqi president tried to enlist

An M109 155-mm (6.1-inch) self-propelled howitzer moves along the dock in preparation for boarding a transport vessel for movement to the Persian Gulf region.

religion into the Iraqi cause. On August 10, therefore, he called for an Arab holy war against the U.S. forces in the region. Given the resentment of many Arabs to the influence of the United States in local affairs, this effort should have stood a better chance of dividing the camp opposing the Iraqis, but in fact it achieved very little. At first, there were signs that Saddam Hussein had hit the right anti-American chord in many Arab hearts, for on August 11 pro-Iraqi demonstrations began in the occupied West Bank of Israel, Jordan, Libya, and Yemen. The wave of anti-American protest soon died away, however, and it was only in Jordan that it lasted more than a few days. Even there, there were indications that the protests were a response not just to anti-American feelings but also to fears about the country's economy, which was largely dependent on trade with Iraq.

Saddam Hussein must have been conscious of the long-term effect that the United Nations' embargo would have on his country and its ability to withstand a sustained campaign, but in the short term

he tried to make propaganda capital out of the situation. In an effort on August 12 to convince other Arab countries that the Western world and its "Arab lackeys" in Saudi Arabia were trying to starve Iraq into submission, Saddam Hussein urged his people to eat less and he called for the lifting of the embargo.

At the same time, the Iraqi president called for all foreign forces to leave Saudi Arabia and be replaced by a pan-Arab force without any Egyptian contingent. Yet he was merely mouthing platitudes. In another utterance, he offered to pull Iraqi forces out of Kuwait in return for the withdrawal of Israel from its occupied territories, and the evacuation of Syrian forces from Lebanon.

On August 13, an Iraqi supertanker was turned away from the Saudi Arabian port of Mu'ajjiz, a major oil terminal on the Red Sea, in clear evidence that the embargo on Iraq was beginning to affect the country's most important export. Yet even at this steadily deteriorating stage, Iraq was not entirely without friends, or at least well-disposed

Opposite: A moment of pensive worry for a small girl as her father departs for the Persian Gulf.

Above: A sailor bids farewell to his wife before embarking on his ship at the Naval Station Norfolk, Virginia, for the journey to the Persian Gulf.

Right: A mother weeps and holds her daughter after her husband, a man of the 24th Infantry Division (Mechanized), has embarked for the Persian Gulf at Hunter Army Airfield, Georgia.

neutrals. King Hussein of Jordan visited Baghdad in another effort to make Saddam Hussein appreciate the true nature of events. As might have been expected, the king's effort was to no avail, but on the following day he traveled to the United States for talks with the Bush administration.

On the same day, Saddam Hussein accused the U.S. of "flagrant piracy," and the United States rejected the suggestion that its warships in the theater should be reflagged under United Nations colors.

Iraqi Peace with Iran

A more threatening event took place on August 15, when Iraq concluded a peace agreement with Iran, finally ending the war that had racked the two countries and recently ended in an armistice. The peace accord recognized Iranian rights on the Shatt-al-Arab waterway and laid the foundations for an exchange of prisoners of war. This latter was particularly important for Iraq, for it removed the need to accommodate, feed, and guard many thousands of Iranian prisoners. At the same time, the morale of the country improved as Iraqi prisoners returned and often rejoined the army. Peace also freed Iraq from the threat of war along its long eastern frontier and allowed the large-scale redeployment of Iraqi forces. Saddam Hussein was worried that trouble could still perhaps flare in this quarter, and he left sizable forces in place along the frontier with Iran. These, and those guarding the frontier with Turkey, were lower-grade forces, however, which freed the army formations

With its turret traversed to the rear to keep the long barrel of the main gun out of the way, an M1 Abrams main battle tank moves up the ramp onto the vehicle/cargo rapid-response ship U.S.N.S. *Regulus*. This is one of an eight-strong class of converted SL-7 civilian cargo ships with a speed of 33 knots and 185,000 square feet of vehicle space.

Above: A McDonnell Douglas F-15C Eagle multi-role fighter of the 27th Tactical Fighter Squadron, 1st Tactical Fighter Wing, in flight over southern Iraq.

Right: An aircraft mechanic of the VAW-125 squadron poses with a Grumman E-2C Hawkeye airborne warning and control airplane on the flight deck of the carrier U.S.S. *Saratoga* in the Persian Gulf.

This McDonnell Douglas AH-64A Apache helicopter of the 101st Aviation Brigade is loaded with AGM-114 Hellfire anti-tank missiles and launchers for 2·75-inch (70-mm) rockets. Also visible are the trainable 30-mm defense-suppression cannon under the fuselage.

with the most modern equipment and best battle record for movement toward southern Iraq and Kuwait. These formations included the divisions of the elite Republican Guard, which received better pay than other army formations, as well as superior equipment and training. Thus the Republican Guard, generally believed to offer a far higher level of combat threat than the ordinary formations of the Iraqi army, was bound personally to Saddam Hussein.

The Infamous "Human Shield" Policy

The next phase of the steady descent to war started on August 16, when Iraq began to implement its "human shield"

policy involving civilians of the countries aligned against it. Most of these civilians were men in Iraq working under civil contracts to provide technical aid to this rapidly developing country, and many of the men with longer-term contracts had their families with them. The rules of international dispute demanded that such civilians be repatriated to their own countries or, failing that, to neutral countries, with an alternative of internment in safe areas for those who would not be repatriated, in the event that hostilities broke out. Iraq had other ideas, however.

On August 15, the U.S.S.R. announced that 5,000 Soviet citizens had been refused permission to leave Iraq. The following day, the situation became clearer when the Iraqi government or-

The Secretary of Defense during the war with Iraq was Richard Cheney.

dered 2,500 American and 4,000 British civilians to report to specified hotels or face arrest. Many refused to heed the Iraqi demand, and those who did respond found no Iraqi officials at the hotels in question. The next day, the motive for this Iraqi move became plain. The Iraqi government revealed that it was detaining the citizens of "aggressive nations" and would accommodate them at key military installations as "human shields" against attacks by the forces of the powers gathering their strength against Iraq. This blatant flouting of normal diplomatic behavior proved a serious mistake. It raised an intense anger in the countries whose citizens were being held and never seriously threatened the belief that if necessary the targets would be attacked

in any case. As the British foreign minister put it, Iraq was resorting to "the tactics of the outlaw."

Adding insult to injury, on August 18, Iraq announced that the first victims of the food shortages that must inevitably affect Iraq would be the country's foreign "guests" including women, children, and babies. The United Nations' Security Council demanded that Iraq permit foreigners to depart from its soil, but Iraq completely ignored this demand where Westerners were concerned. It is worth noting, however, that there was a large-scale exodus from the country by the non-Iraqi Arab population. This tragic exodus received no support from the Iraqi authorities, and many died or suffered acute hardship as they fled toward

Opposite: Men of the U.S. Marine Corps detachment on board U.S.S. *Independence* exercise on the carrier's flight deck in front of McDonnell Douglas F/A-18C Hornet dual-role fighter.

Below: Female members of the U.S. Army played an invaluable role in the war with Iraq. They were carefully briefed on the different role played by women in Saudi Arabia.

Jordan across the inhospitable desert. It was estimated that by August 18, 100,000 Arabs had managed to flee Iraq in anticipation of the eventual war.

Tentative Military Sparring

Already the first military moves had started. On August 16, the pilots of U.S. Navy fighter aircraft operating on the Persian Gulf reported that on several occasions they had secured a radar "lock" on Iraqi aircraft, in all probability French-supplied Dassault-Breguet Mirage F1 attack fighters armed with Exocet antiship missiles. The Gulf was the region that inevitably held the greatest dangers

of an early spark, and on August 18, an American destroyer, U.S.S. *Reid*, fired shots across the bows of two Iraqi tankers, both empty, but believed to be looking for a port where they could take on a fresh cargo of oil.

Iraqi Threat of "Mass Destruction"

More tinder was added to the beginnings of the blaze on August 17, when it was reported in the Iraqi press that Iraq was ready to use weapons of "mass destruction." These weapons remained unspecified, but Western intelligence was sure that they did not yet include nuclear

weapons. It was known that Iraq was making good progress in a frantic program to develop nuclear weapons, but even the most pessimistic analysts agreed that Iraq was still at least two years from perfecting a nuclear capability. The alternative lay in chemical and biological weapons, and Iraq was known to possess both types. The country already had a history of using one of these dreadful weapons; during the war with Iran, chemical warheads were used on the battlefield.

More worrying by far to those coordinating the growing effort against Iraq was the knowledge that Saddam Hussein cared so little for humanity that he had also ordered the use of chemical weapons against other Iraqis. Over many years, the Kurds of northern Iraq have tried to establish a Kurdish homeland independent of Iraq, or at least autonomous within Iraq; and on several occasions, Iraqi forces had used chemical weapons against Kurdish villages and towns thought to harbor dissidents. These episodes had been well publicized,

and Western television crews had recorded the scenes in which the bodies of women and children littered otherwise peaceful scenes.

The fact that Saddam Hussein certainly had no moral objection to the use of such weapons was a factor that had to be taken carefully into account by the planners of what was now becoming an allied force of promised international contingents. Best prepared to face such a threat were American and British forces, which had long had to face a Soviet threat of chemical weapons in the European theater, and some of the other allies had modest if not good capabilities against chemical warfare. The problem was a double one, for it required not only the provision of the right equipment (special masks and all-over protective suits, as well as detection and decontamination gear), but also training in its use. The protective equipment had been designed with the moderate European climate in mind and was poorly adapted to the demands of desert

Above: Task Force 155 was one of the U.S. Navy's most important operational groupings in the Middle East at the time of the crisis and war with Iraq. Abreast from left to right, they are the cruiser U.S.S. *Thomas S. Gates*, the aircraft carrier U.S.S. *Saratoga*, the cruiser U.S.S. *San Jacinto*, the aircraft carrier U.S.S. *John F. Kennedy* (flagship), the nuclear-powered cruiser U.S.S. *Mississippi*, the aircraft carrier U.S.S. *America*, the destroyer U.S.S. *William V. Pratt*, the cruiser U.S.S. *Normandy*, the cruiser U.S.S. *Philippine Sea*, and the destroyer U.S.S. *Preble*.

warfare that might erupt in the hottest part of the year. Yet practice and more practice meant that the soldiers could scramble into their protective suits within moments of an alarm and then function with some efficiency for at least a couple of hours before heat and thirst degraded their capabilities.

The "Scud" Factor

It was not only in the front line that the threat of chemical warfare had to be considered. Iraq possessed artillery that could fire chemical-laden shells on the battlefield. In addition, it had a significant number of Soviet-supplied "Scud" surface-to-surface missiles that could be fitted with chemical warheads for attacks on military rear areas. Experts also knew that Iraq had produced two developments of the basic "Scud" for greater ranges with smaller payloads, and these existing missiles opened up the terrible possibility of Iraqi chemical attacks on distant civilian targets.

As these factors were being taken into account, reports were beginning to emerge from Kuwait of Iraqi atrocities. From the earliest days of the occupation, Iraqi forces were systematically looting the country, not only of national resources and treasures, but also of basic consumer goods. An emerging resistance movement in Kuwait was beginning to

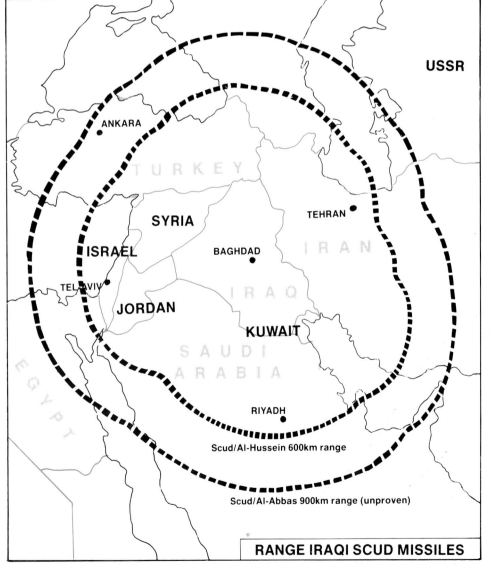

Scud/Al-Hussein 600km range

Scud/Al-Abbas 900km range (unproven)

RANGE IRAQI SCUD MISSILES

make its presence felt, and the Iraqis responded with a steady brutalization of their regime, which rounded up, tortured, and killed Kuwaiti civilians. On August 19, the Iraqi administration ordered all Westerners in Kuwait to report to designated hotels, or face the dangers of being rounded up by troops. Most of the Westerners left in Kuwait were British, and the British government advised them by radio not to comply with the Iraqi order. Even so, on the first day of the Iraqi round-up, 82 British citizens were seized, in addition to another 41 who had previously been detained.

Diplomacy Matched by Armed Preparation

As the diplomatic effort against Saddam Hussein continued, allied military preparations for a war of Kuwaiti liberation continued. From the beginning,

A Lockheed F-117A "Stealth" warplane of the 37th Tactical Fighter Wing takes on fuel from a McDonnell Douglas KC-10A Extender tanker of the 22nd Air Refueling Wing, normally based at March Air Force Base, California.

President Bush and his military advisers decided that if Iraq refused to pull back, military effort would have to be used. The prospect of large-scale operations in this classic fighting country opened the possibility of casualties on a large scale, however. In an effort to keep losses as low as possible, the administration and the Department of Defense agreed that American forces should use all the high-technology weapons and systems available to them. As part of this plan, the president on August 20 ordered the deployment of 20 Lockheed F-117A "Stealth" aircraft. These planes, designed to avoid detection by the types of Soviet air-defense radar used by the Iraqis, were expected to play a decisive part through their ability to reach high-value targets and destroy them with precision weapons such as air-to-surface missiles and laser-guided bombs. Other U.S. warplanes possessed this capability to a lesser

extent, and the commanders hoped that the deployment of this aircraft would make it possible, in the event of hostilities with Iraq, to destroy railroad lines, bridges, tunnels, and ammunition dumps, as well as command and communication centers. The first breach of the United Nations' embargo on trade with Iraq was reported on August 21; it was revealed that an Iraqi tanker was unloading in the Yemeni port of Aden. Such breaches were in fact very few, but the Yemeni acceptance of this load angered the Saudi Arabians particularly and led ultimately to the expulsion of many thousands of Yemenis living and working in Saudi Arabia. The refugee problem was beginning to hit Jordan very badly, and on August 22, Jordan closed its border with Iraq to prevent the arrival of a further flood of refugees.

On the same day, President Bush authorized the mobilization of 40,000

Lockheed F-117A "Stealth" warplanes of the 37th Tactical Fighter Wing present a highly unusual appearance at Langley Air Force Base, Virginia, as they stage on their way from Tonopah Test Range Airfield (part of the Nellis Air Force Base complex in Nevada) to Saudi Arabia.

reservists, many of them technicians and medical personnel, who were expected to make a particularly important contribution if the desert war started.

Increasing Tension in Kuwait

Iraqi troops surrounded the surviving Western embassies in Kuwait on August 24, beginning an effort to force diplomatic personnel to leave Kuwait and move to Baghdad. Gradually, the Iraqis tightened their net around the embassies, cutting off their water and electricity supplies. The embassies had already thinned their staffs to absolute minimum figures, and they now faced the problems of surviving as long as possible on stored food and water from their swimming pools. On the same

day, Soviet President Mikhail Gorbachev urged Iraq to pull out of Kuwait, adding that any refusal to do so would inevitably cause the United Nations to take "additional measures." The U.S.S.R. also evacuated the last of its citizens from Kuwait.

Faced with total intransigence on the part of Saddam Hussein, the United Nations on August 25 agreed to the eventual use of force against the Iraqi forces. With events taking an even steeper downhill path, there was a redoubled diplomatic effort to solve the problem. On August 25, President Kurt Waldheim of Austria, who had been secretary general of the United Nations Organization, met Saddam Hussein in Baghdad, but failed to make any headway. On August 26, Xavier Perez de Cuellar, the current secretary general, announced that he would try to mediate in

Lockheed F-117A warplanes of the 37th Tactical Fighter Wing's 416th Tactical Fighter Squadron turn off the main runway after landing at their Saudi Arabian base.

The cooperative effort in the Persian Gulf buildup is epitomized as Sergeant Eugene E. Jiggitss, an air traffic controller with the 2nd Combat Communications Group at Patrick Air Force Base, Florida, shares control of inbound traffic with a Saudi Arabian officer, 1st Lieutenant Saled M. Shahrani.

the dispute, and King Hussein launched a further personal initiative with a visit to Libya, one of the few countries to have declared an open support for Iraq and thus thought to offer a favorable line of access to Saddam Hussein.

Yet the situation in the Middle East deteriorated even more, when, on the same day, the Iraqi administration announced its intention to hang anyone found harboring a Westerner in Iraq or Kuwait.

End of the "Human Shield" Policy

Over the following week, diplomatic efforts continued, but they failed to break into the problem, let alone solve it. The one positive move occurred on August 28, when Saddam Hussein finally realized the futility of his "human shield" policy. He announced that women and children "guests" were free to leave Iraq, a process that began on September 2 when a Boeing 747 arrived at London's Heathrow Airport with 200 British women and children. Yet on the same day, the maverick in international circles, Colonel Gaddafi of Libya, made the impossible promise to supply Iraq with food and fuel by means of a "bridge" of air transports. On September 3, the Iraqi administration urged British women and children still hiding in Kuwait to come out of concealment and join a convoy to Baghdad. One day later, a convoy of coaches carrying 300 Western women and children reached Baghdad.

Despite some positive moves, Saddam Hussein was still completely unwilling to negotiate on the real issues, and hopes of continued peace began to fade. Talks were held, starting on September 6 in Riyadh, between Secretary of State James Baker and the Saudi Arabian government

about who could authorize the start of operations against the Iraqis. These discussions took place just after the U.S. marines in Saudi Arabia moved farther north after completing a series of static defenses designed to check any Iraqi advance into Saudi Arabia.

A Superpower Summit

The crisis was accompanied by an unusual degree of cooperation between the United States and the U.S.S.R., and on September 9, Presidents Bush and Gorbachev met in Helsinki, the capital of Finland, for a summit about the Kuwaiti situation. The two leaders agreed that the Iraqis must leave Kuwait, but disagreed on how to achieve this goal. Gorbachev wished to give diplomacy and the United Nations' embargo a greater chance, but Bush was increasingly convinced that

Saddam Hussein would never listen to reason. U.S. forces in the Persian Gulf region totaled 100,000 men and large quantities of equipment, and the threat of a preemptive Iraqi strike were fading.

One day later, Secretary Baker appealed to the North Atlantic Treaty Organization for military support, but received little more than token offers The two Arab "superpowers," Egypt and Syria, were making a more important physical contribution, the small Gulf states were providing what they could, and on September 7 Saudi Arabia increased its physical contribution by offering considerable financial support to the allied effort. On the other side of the fence, Saddam Hussein offered third-world countries free oil if they could arrange to move it, but this open attempt to break the embargo on trade with Iraq was a total failure. Iran restored diplomatic relations with Iraq, but agreed

A fish-eye view of the flight deck on a Boeing KC-135 Stratotanker over Saudi Arabia during Operation "Desert Shield." The inflight refueling capability of these old but invaluable tankers played a major part in Operation "Desert Storm," allowing warplanes to roam deep into Iraq.

James Baker
For further references
see pages
78, 82

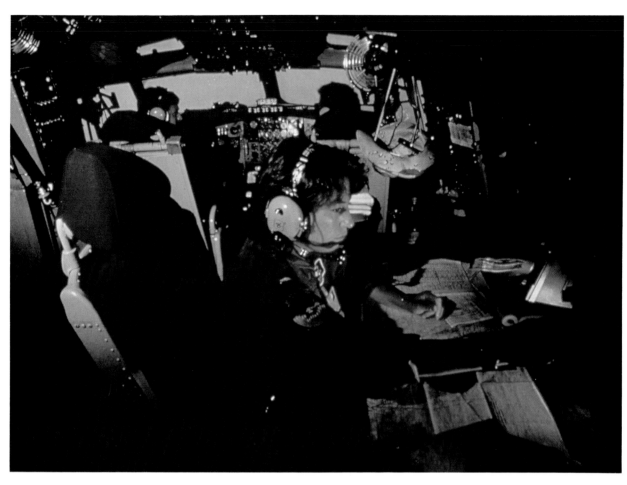

not to break the embargo in any way.

Thereafter, the slide toward war continued against a backdrop of misguided and ultimately futile efforts at mediation. A few noteworthy events occurred in mid-September. The British embassy in Kuwait finally closed on September 13 as its stocks of food ran out. The following day, it was announced that a British armored brigade would be moved from Germany to Saudi Arabia. On September 14, the French embassy in Kuwait was invaded by Iraqi troops, and the French government announced that 4,000 French troops would be sent to Saudi Arabia. The opening of the Kuwaiti frontier with Saudi Arabia by the Iraqis on September 16 resulted in a flood of Kuwaiti refugees going south.

Terrorist Intervention?

On September 18, George Habash of the extremist Popular Front for the Libera-

tion of Palestine, said that his group had "fingers on triggers and shall shoot American and Western targets the moment the U.S. attacks Iraq." The specter of resurgent terrorism at an international level had an immediate and unusually long-lasting effect on the previously booming airline industry. Many thousands of booked flights – to places all over the world – were cancelled and not reinstated. The possible expansion of the conflict was also foreshadowed by the Israeli prime minister, Yitzhak Shamir, when he announced on September 20 that Israel would fight Iraq alone if the United States backed down. Three days later, Iraq responded with the threat to destroy Israel and the Saudi Arabian oilfields if the allied forces tried to "strangle" Iraq.

Two days later, the Security Council voted for an air embargo on Iraq, and on the same day the Soviet foreign minister, Eduard Shevardnadze, told the United Nations that the U.S.S.R. would not back

Logistic support for Operations "Desert Shield" and "Desert Storm" involved a huge effort by transport aircraft such as the Lockheed C-141 Star Lifter. On the flight deck of this transport, a female captain is seen at the navigation station.

the use of force to expel the Iraqis from Kuwait. Still belatedly trying to recover some credit from its ill-advised "human shield" policy, Iraq announced on October 23 that it would free all 330 of its French hostages, and on the same day 33 British "guests" were released to return to the United Kingdom with ex-Prime Minister Edward Heath, another of the international figures convinced that a non-violent solution to the Kuwaiti problem could be negotiated. On November 8, Saddam Hussein threatened to reduce the Arabian peninsula to ashes, and President Bush authorized the movement of another 100,000 American service personnel to the area.

The UN Authorizes the Use of Force

The next decisive moment occurred on November 29, when the Security Council passed a resolution authorizing the allied forces to use direct military means to oust the Iraqi forces from Kuwait if they remained in the country after a deadline

With two of its four AIM-9M Sidewinder short-range air-to-air missiles highly visible, this General Dynamics F-16 Fighting Falcon awaits maintenance at a Saudi Arabian air base.

set for January 15, 1991. Another round of diplomatic efforts followed, but again failed. The major effort was made by President Bush, who on November 30 invited Tariq Aziz, the Iraqi foreign minister, to Washington and suggested that Secretary of State Baker visit Baghdad to leave Saddam Hussein in no doubt that the United States really meant business. This was a sincere – but perhaps misguided – effort on the president's part, for Saddam Hussein claimed that the United States had now changed its basic policy and said that Iraq had gained a "triumph." One day later Saddam Hussein accepted the American offer – on the condition that the Israeli/Palestinian problem be part of the agenda.

On December 6, Iraq finally announced the release of its last hostages.

The Iraqi government tried to arrange Secretary Baker's visit to Baghdad for January 12, 1991, and on December

11 Washington claimed that this Iraqi delay was merely a ploy to push back the United Nations' deadline. Four days later, Tariq Aziz replied that he would not visit Washington. The effort at negotiation seemed fated to a stalemate, and on December 17 President Bush insisted that any talks would have to be completed by the January 15 deadline set by the United Nations.

Time for a settlement was now running out quickly, and on December 22 the situation was made tenser still. Saddam Hussein issued a declaration that Kuwait would forever be part of Iraq and that any attack would result in the Iraqi use of chemical weapons. A meeting between Secretary Baker and Tariq Aziz was finally scheduled for January 9 in Geneva, but failed to produce any concrete result. Throughout this period, moreover, Saddam Hussein continued to issue provocative statements. On January 6, he said

President and Mrs. Bush arrive in Saudi Arabia to spend Thanksgiving with American personnel involved in Operation "Desert Shield."

U.S. marines gather at a desert camp in preparation for a Thanksgiving visit by President Bush.

that Iraq would make any sacrifice necessary to retain Kuwait and free Palestine and, on January 11, that a "showdown between infidels and believers" was imminent. Despite these attempts to break the cohesion of the allied camp by bringing Israel and Islam into the reckoning, Saddam achieved no result of the slightest use to Iraq as the clock ran down to zero hour.

Wasted Diplomatic Efforts

As the ultimately futile diplomatic process continued, a huge logistic effort was moving vast numbers of personnel and still vaster quantities of materiel into the area. Despite the relatively short time available and the head start provided by the equipment forward-stocked for the Central Command, the American buildup soon overtook the Berlin airlift and the deployments to Korea and Vietnam, and remains unbeaten in modern times except by the transoceanic movement of men and equipment in World War II. As early as the end of August 1990, the scale of the transportation effort was graphically described as being equivalent to the weight of 400,000 automobiles. Hundreds of ships and aircraft were involved in a complex but carefully coordinated movement pattern, carrying items as varied as battle tanks and packs of cigarettes. By the time of the United

Above: President Bush addresses personnel of the U.S. Marine Corps and U.S. Navy at a desert encampment during his Thanksgiving visit to Saudi Arabia.

Right: The look of American power against Iraq: an American soldier on guard duty "somewhere in Saudi Arabia."

Nations' deadline, the ships and aircraft of the allied logistic apparatus had covered 58 million miles.

By the same date, U.S. troops were getting through one million meals and 700 tons of mail every day, and the nature of the climate had resulted in the delivery of 551,000 bottles of sunscreen lotion and 715,000 containers of foot powder. Right across the United States, service storage areas were being emptied; and some indication of the scale of consumption is provided by a single ship. The aircraft carrier U.S.S. *John F. Kennedy* received 3½ million gallons of fuel and 22,000 tons of food.

The Iraqi Forces

On the eve of hostilities, the Iraqis had gathered a very substantial array of men and equipment in the region. Under the overall command of Saddam Hussein, the Iraqi forces were supervised by Lieutenant General Hussein Rashid, the chief of staff, and Major General Saadi Tumas Abbas, the defense minister. The

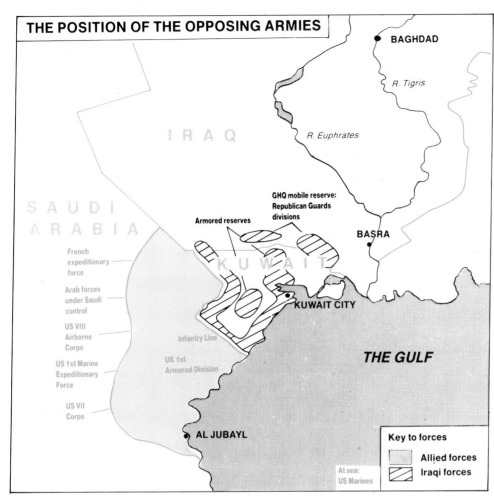

THE POSITION OF THE OPPOSING ARMIES

BAGHDAD

R. Tigris

I R A Q

R. Euphrates

GHQ mobile reserve:
Republican Guards
divisions

Armored reserves

BASRA

S A U D I
A R A B I A

French
expeditionary
force

Arab forces
under Saudi
control

K U W A I T

US VIII
Airborne
Corps

Infantry Line

US 1st Marine
Expeditionary
Force

UK 1st
Armored Division

US VII
Corps

KUWAIT CITY

THE GULF

AL JUBAYL

Key to forces

Allied forces
Iraqi forces

At sea:
US Marines

This map details the
basic positions of the
opposing forces
during the period of
Operation "Desert
Shield."

two were the most recent incumbents of their offices, for senior officers were either fired or executed frequently as they fell out of favor with Saddam Hussein for military or political reasons. Between the Iraqi invasion of Kuwait and the start of hostilities, there had been four rounds of removal and promotion. Hussein Rashid had commanded the Republican Guard in 1985-86, then commanded I Corps in 1986-87, and in 1987 became deputy chief of staff for operations before being elevated to his current position.

The Iraqi forces facing the allies included some 590,000 men (including 350,000 in Kuwait) with 4,300 tanks, 2,900 other armored fighting vehicles, 3,100 pieces of artillery, 500 fixed-wing aircraft, and 200 battlefield helicopters. The Iraqi ground forces facing the allies totaled 38 divisions. Of these, the best were the seven Republican Guard divisions being held back just inside Iraq itself as the general reserve. The

Republican Guard formations were divided into two groups centered on Umm Qasr in the east and Halaybah in the west. Of the ordinary divisions, the infantry formations were deployed along the frontier in a cordon defense that stretched from al Bahrah on Kuwait's northeastern coast right around the eastern, southern, and southwestern borders to a point just inside Iraq from Kuwait's western end. The armored divisions were held back as immediate reserve and, like the Republican Guards, were divided into two groups centered on al Jahrah and as Sabiriyah in the center and north of the country respectively.

The Iraqi navy, with only 14 small warships, was a negligible factor.

The Allies Gather

The allies included elements from no fewer than 33 countries, though many

**Republican
Guard**
For further references
see pages
68, 109

Charles Horner
For further references
see pages
95, *98*, 100

The 82nd Aviation
Brigade's Sikorsky
UH-60 Black Hawk
utility transport
helicopters are on
view at the unit's base
in the Saudi Arabian
desert before the
beginning of Operation
"Desert Storm."

of these were little more than token contributions. The ground forces totaled 690,000 troops with 3,500 tanks, very large numbers of other armored fighting vehicles, 1,800 pieces of artillery, 1,900 fixed-wing aircraft, and 800 battlefield helicopters. The allied navy was not a negligible factor, for it had some 160 warships to the Iraqis 15.

Of this allied force, the largest ground-force contingent by far was that of the United States, which contributed 350,000 fighting men and women and 2,000 tanks. Other allied components were provided by the United Kingdom (Lieutenant General Sir Peter de la Billiere's 27,000 troops with 160 tanks), Saudi Arabia (20,000 troops with 200 tanks), Egypt (Lieutenant General M. al Halaby's 30,000 troops with 300 tanks), Syria (Major General A. Habib's 20,000 troops with 200 tanks), France

(General Michel Roquejoffre's 16,000 troops), Kuwait (7,000 troops), Pakistan (5,000 troops), Bangladesh (2,000 troops), Morocco (1,200 troops), Senegal (500 troops), Niger (500 troops), and the Gulf Co-Operation Council states (3,000 troops from Bahrain, Oman, Qatar, and the United Arab Emirates).

In the air, the U.S. effort also predominated. In addition to 48 Boeing B-52 Stratofortress heavy bombers, there were 1,000 land-based and carrierborne aircraft available to the command headed by Lieutenant General Charles Horner. Other allied contributions included 138 Saudi Arabian, 60 British, 38 French, and 15 Kuwaiti aircraft. At sea, too, the American effort was the largest, with six aircraft carriers carrying 360 warplanes, two battleships, some 55 other warships and amphibious warfare vessels, and 23 support vessels under the command of

Vice Admiral Stanley Arthur. Other allied contributions came from the British (four warships as well as 11 support vessels and minesweepers), the French (six warships and three support vessels), and the other allies (31 warships and support vessels).

A Huge American Contribution

In greater detail, the American commitment to the land forces included about 275,000 army troops, including some 90,000 reservists and National Guardsmen, and 45,000 marines. Shortly before the expiry of the United Nations' deadline, the area just inside the Saudi Arabian/Kuwaiti border was held by Arab forces under the overall Saudi Arabian command of Prince Khaled bin Sultan,

with Lieutenant General Abdul Rahman as his field commander. Behind this cordon force was the main weight of the American ground forces.

As far south as al Jubayl and as far west as the edge of the southward projection of Kuwait into Saudi Arabia, the coastal region was held by the 1st Marine Expeditionary Force under the command of Lieutenant General Walter Boomer and included the 4th and 5th Marine Amphibious Brigades and the 1st Marine Amphibious Force. The marines were short of modern armored strength, and for this reason had under command the British contingent, made up of Major General Rupert Smith's 1st Armored Division of the 4th and 7th Armoured Brigades, whose Challenger tanks gave the British and marine formation a powerful armored capability;

M551 Sheridan light tanks of the 82nd Airborne Division move toward the firing range for a live-firing exercise during the closing stages of Operation "Desert Shield."

As Operation "Desert Shield" built up the forces that would be needed for Operation "Desert Storm," boredom among the troops became a factor to be taken into account by the American commanders. Saudi Arabia offered little opportunity for the types of diversions generally enjoyed by the American forces, and personnel had to spend considerable time in their tents sheltering from the burning sun and finding what entertainment they could.

the 1st Armoured Division held the northwestern corner of the marine zone where it joined the U.S. army zone.

Farther inland, holding the zone to the south and, more importantly, to the west of the marines, in the region where Iraq and Saudi Arabia share a border, were the army forces. The ground force commander was Lieutenant General John Yeosock, who had considerable experience of the region after spending the early 1980s in Saudi Arabia as an adviser on the modernization of the Saudi Arabian national guard. The formations under Yeosock's command were, from east to west, Lieutenant General Fred Franks's VII Corps and Lieutenant General Gary Luck's XVIII Airborne Corps. The former included the 1st and 3rd Armored Divisions and the 1st Infantry Divisions, while the latter controlled the 82nd and 101st Airborne Divisions, the 1st Cavalry

Division, and the 24th Mechanized Infantry Division.

Complex Yet Effective Command Structure

Command of this huge force was a complex affair, and for political reasons supreme command was notionally exercised by Prince Khaled bin Sultan, who was responsible to Prince Sultan ibn Abdul Aziz, the Saudi Arabian defense minister, and ultimately to King Fahd. Real command was entrusted as a result of cooperation agreements to an American officer, General Norman Schwarzkopf, the commander of all American forces in the area in his capacity as the Commander, Middle East. Schwarzkopf's next-in-command was Lieutenant General Calvin Waller, aged 53, and previously commander of I Corps.

General Norman Schwarzkopf, commander of Central Command.

Aged 56, Schwarzkopf is a true "soldier's soldier." In the Vietnam War, he served first as an adviser to the South Vietnamese airborne division and then as a battalion commander in the 23rd Infantry Division. He is also an expert in desert warfare, having trained regularly in the Mojave Desert and in Egypt, and was assistant commander of the American operation to take Grenada before moving

The military effort in Washington was run by General Colin Powell, chairman of the Joint Chiefs of Staff.

to the Pentagon as deputy chief of staff for operations and plans.

In Washington, control of the U.S. military effort was exercised by Richard Cheney, the Secretary of Defense, and General Colin Powell, the chairman of the Joint Chiefs of Staff. When he arrived in Saudi Arabia on August 26 to establish his command headquarters and plan for the removal of the Iraqi occupiers from Kuwait, Schwarzkopf already had many notions of how this objective might be attained. Schwarzkopf's primary aim was to achieve this end swiftly and decisively, but at minimum cost to the allies. The clearest way was massive use of the allies' technological superiority, initially by the air forces.

First Step: A Huge Air Offensive

In overall terms, the initial stage of the allied campaign against Iraq was therefore based on a massive air effort that was planned with several major, but generally equal, objectives. The first was the severing of all Iraqi land communications with Kuwait, thereby isolating the Iraqi land forces in that area from

Norman Schwarzkopf
For further references see pages
88, *89*, 95, *101*, *102*, 109, 112, 113, 116, 117, 119, 120, 131

Colin Powell
For further references see pages
100, *101*, *119*, 120

reinforcement and resupply. This part of the campaign involved the destruction of all roads and railroads that could be used by the Iraqis, together with key chokepoints such as bridges and tunnels. The second objective was the destruction of the Iraqi Air Force, in the air if need be, but preferably on the ground, by the use of guided weapons to destroy hardened aircraft shelters, and cratering bombs to destroy the runways that would be needed by any surviving aircraft. The third objective was the elimination of Iraq's nuclear and chemical warfare capabilities by the destruction of research and production facilities, again through the use of precision-guided weapons. The final aim was the destruction of the

command and control systems by which the Iraqi high command supervised the war effort, which again involved the employment of precision-guided weapons, including General Dynamics BGM-109 Tomahawk cruise missiles fired from warships in the Red Sea and Persian Gulf to cripple command bunkers, ruin power stations, and stop broadcasts; this last would also have the useful effect of reducing the flow of Saddam Hussein's propaganda to the Iraqi people.

Together with these specific objectives, the allied air forces were tasked with harassing the everyday life of Iraq in all manner of ways, generally using conventional weapons. It was very

In the years before its invasion of Kuwait, Iraq had built up its armed forces and their logistical infrastructure. Recognizing that air power is one of the keys to success in modern warfare, the Iraqis contracted Western companies for large numbers of hardened aircraft shelters (HASs). When hostilities broke out, they became a major target for allied attack aircraft.

clearly established that extreme accuracy of targeting was essential, not only to guarantee the destruction of planned targets, but also to minimize civilian casualties. This was particularly important to the free-roving aircraft, whose task of general harassment was combined with the very important specific role of eliminating the Iraqi antiaircraft capability. This latter was based on the Soviet pattern and used a combination of radars and weapons (antiaircraft guns of all calibers and surface-to-air missiles) operating in several overlapping layers, and its destruction would give aircraft attacking the major objectives a better chance of attacking accurately and escaping safely.

Operation "Desert Storm" Starts

The first part of the shooting war that began on January 17 was the air campaign. Well over 1,000 aircraft were launched on the first wave of at-tacks, dropping some 2,230 tons of ordnance on targets all over Iraq. The aircrews secured virtually complete tactical surprise, and the allied electronic warfare systems degraded the Iraqi air-defense capability to a remarkable degree. Even so, the defenses put up a mass of antiaircraft artillery fire and large numbers of surface-to-air missiles, but managed to knock down only one plane, a McDonnell Douglas F/A-18 Hornet attack fighter. The luckiest escape of this first effort was that of a McDonnell Douglas F-4G Phantom II involved in a "Wild Weasel" operation against an Iraqi air-defense complex: no fewer than six surface-to-air missiles were launched against this single two-seat plane, and its pilot had to use all his flying skills and a fair measure of luck to evade the missiles.

The air campaign continued steadily over the following days, and allied aircrews were amazed that they were encountering virtually no opposition in the air; the Iraqi Air Force's surviving aircraft were hidden from allied

Men and women of the American forces take a meal break in the Saudi Arabian desert.

Left: Part of the mechanized force play their part in the deep movement to outflank the Iraqi army in Kuwait during the 100-hour land campaign of Operation "Desert Storm."

Below: An M1 Abrams main battle tank of the 24th Infantry Division (Mechanized) patrols in the region just south of the Saudi Arabian border with occupied Kuwait, its crew watchful for any sign of an Iraqi offensive designed to disrupt allied preparations.

The 100-hour land offensive of Operation "Desert Storm."

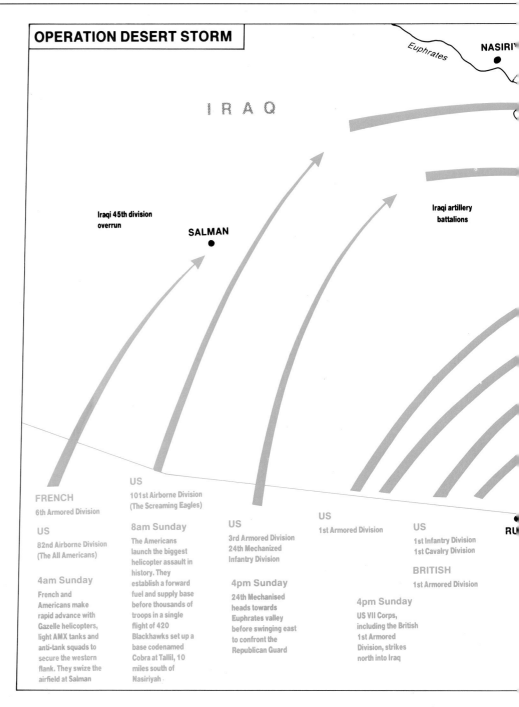

OPERATION DESERT STORM

Euphrates

NASIRI

IRAQ

Iraqi 45th division
overrun

SALMAN

Iraqi artillery
battalions

FRENCH
6th Armored Division

US
82nd Airborne Division
(The All Americans)

4am Sunday

French and
Americans make
rapid advance with
Gazelle helicopters,
light AMX tanks and
anti-tank squads to
secure the western
flank. They swize the
airfield at Salman

US
101st Airborne Division
(The Screaming Eagles)

8am Sunday

The Americans
launch the biggest
helicopter assault in
history. They
establish a forward
fuel and supply base
before thousands of
troops in a single
flight of 420
Blackhawks set up a
base codenamed
Cobra at Tallil, 10
miles south of
Nasiriyah

US
3rd Armored Division
24th Mechanized
Infantry Division

4pm Sunday

24th Mechanised
heads towards
Euphrates valley
before swinging east
to confront the
Republican Guard

US
1st Armored Division

US
1st Infantry Division
1st Cavalry Division

BRITISH
1st Armored Division

4pm Sunday

US VII Corps,
including the British
1st Armored
Division, strikes
north into Iraq

RU

reconnaissance and the inevitable sequel of an air attack. Enormous damage to Iraq and its physical infrastructure resulted, and allied air losses were still extraordinarily low, amounting to just 20 aircraft in the first week of the operation.

Another Iraqi Blunder

At this point, Saddam Hussein made another extraordinary propaganda blunder. Captured aircrew were paraded on Iraqi television, and it was announced that these men were to be confined as "human shields" at strategic targets to which the Red Cross would be denied access. It also appeared to observers that these survivors might have been beaten, and possibly tortured, and this impression was highlighted by the deadpan way in which some officers

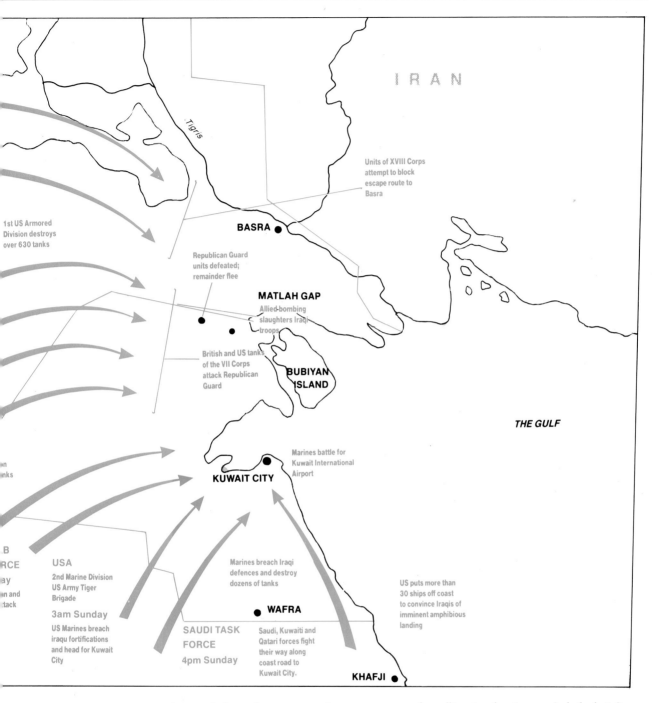

IRAN

Tigris

Units of XVIII Corps
attempt to block
escape route to
Basra

BASRA

1st US Armored
Division destroys
over 630 tanks

Republican Guard
units defeated;
remainder flee

MATLAH GAP
Allied bombing
slaughters Iraqi
troops

British and US tanks
of the VII Corps
attack Republican
Guard

**BUBIYAN
ISLAND**

THE GULF

Marines battle for
Kuwait International
Airport

KUWAIT CITY

US puts more than
30 ships off coast
to convince Iraqis of
imminent amphibious
landing

Marines breach Iraqi
defences and destroy
dozens of tanks

.B
RCE
ay
n and
:tack

USA
2nd Marine Division
US Army Tiger
Brigade

3am Sunday
US Marines breach
iraqu fortifications
and head for Kuwait
City

**SAUDI TASK
FORCE**

4pm Sunday

Saudi, Kuwaiti and
Qatari forces fight
their way along
coast road to
Kuwait City.

WAFRA

KHAFJI

intoned forced propaganda messages. The possibility of such treatment inevitably worried aircrews, but it also made them angry and further inflamed public opinion in the countries of the allied coalition. After this inept Iraqi effort, virtually the last vestiges of opposition to "Desert Storm" ceased in the United States.

An altogether more successful propaganda exercise was undertaken by the allies in the form of daily briefings. The stars were undoubtedly Schwarzkopf and Horner, whose lively, well-presented briefings helped to persuade the news media, and via them the world public, that the allied air campaign was not repeat of the carpet bombing that caused so much devastation in Vietnam and Cambodia, but surgical strikes by highly trained aircrews operating at medium and low levels with precision weapons to

Opposite Top: A Kuwaiti pilot who managed to escape from the invading Iraqis is interviewed in front of his McDonnell Douglas A-4K Skyhawk light attack warplane, which carries a suitable legend on its fuselage side.

Opposite Below: Airmen unload an AIM-9 Sidewinder air-to-air missile from a McDonnell Douglas F-15 Eagle fighter at a Saudi Arabian base. The yellow protector over the nose shields the transparent cover of the missile's infrared seeker unit.

Above: McDonnell Douglas F/A-18 Hornet pilots discuss their mission with crewmen of the U.S.S. *Saratoga* after landing on the carrier.

Left: Inward concentration is evident on the face of this tank driver of the 24th Infantry Division (Mechanized).

Right: Lieutenant General Charles Horner commanded the elements of the U.S. Air Force involved in Operation "Desert Storm."

Below: Another study in concentration: a squad automatic weapon gunner on the ranges during live-firing practice.

the Iraqis war-waging capabilities. The trouble with such briefings, however, was that they helped to persuade the public that the war was all but won when, of course, it was still very far from over, since the Iraqis still held Kuwait. It was therefore decided to play down the successes of the air campaign and to emphasize that this was only the preface to a land war. As President Bush put it: "There will be losses; there will be obstacles along the way. War is never cheap or easy." The U.S. commanders began to talk in terms of at least another 100,000 air sorties before the land war could begin.

American Problems of Interpretation

During this period, there was a growing divergence of opinion between the U.S. commanders in Riyadh and Washington. Those in Saudi Arabia relied on aircrew reports and battle damage assessments, and decided that most of the Iraqi air force had been smashed or rendered impotent on the ground, and that perhaps

destroy specific buildings and installations with minimum collateral damage. The video footage used to illustrate these briefings of course emphasized the successes rather than the failures, but it was nonetheless evident that enormous destruction was being visited on

30 percent of the Iraqi tanks had been destroyed. But those in Washington relied more on satellite reconnaissance and, with the support of the Central Intelligence Agency, said that much of the Iraqi air force was still operative and that less than 10 percent of Iraqi tanks had been destroyed. So far as tanks were concerned, the allies were hoping to destroy 50 percent of the Iraqi armor before launching a ground offensive to retake Kuwait.

The dispute about Iraqi air strength was more academic, for those aircraft that survived the initial onslaught played no further part in the air campaign. Iraq had lost some 20 aircraft in the first phase of the air campaign, and the surviving aircraft were either flown to remote airstrips in the north of the country or parked in residential areas where the allies would not attack them. Even so, the allied air forces continued to approach Iraqi air bases to complete the

Soldiers of the 82nd Airborne Division on the move in the Saudi Arabian desert. In addition to his pack, the man at the rear is also carrying a mortar baseplate, a heavy cast metal piece which supports the base of the weapon to prevent it from sinking into the ground under the force of the recoil.

destruction of their runways and aircraft shelters.

Then on January 26 an extraordinary happening was detected by a Boeing E-3 Sentry airborne warning and control system airplane: Iraqi aircraft were fleeing at low level to Iran. Whether it was a mass defection or a planned evacuation was uncertain, and other such flights were made at later dates. By the end of the war, some 147 of Iraq's best warplanes had reached the safety of Iranian airfields. Whatever the reason, it eased the task of the allied air forces, for the aircraft were interned by the Iranians and were thus removed from the planning.

Even so, the allied air forces continued to fly some 2,500 missions every day under the control of Horner and Brigadier General "Buster" Glosson, Horner's principal target planner. Careful planning, based on extensive satellite reconnaissance and other intelligence, was geared to the specific needs of a clearcut yet flexible operational plan. The campaign of rolling attacks secured allied control of the air by destroying airfields, air-defense radar, and command and control centers. Once they had air superiority, the allied air forces could turn their attention to removing the most immediate threat to the allied land forces, namely the "Scud" missiles and their Iraqi-developed variants, together with their

Opposite Top: The deck of an aircraft carrier is apparently the scene of total confusion during aircraft launch and recovery operations, but the movement of men and machines is in fact a highly orchestrated and complex pattern.

Opposite Below: Secretary of Defense Richard Cheney and General Colin Powell testify before Congress, which was kept fully informed with the development of Operation "Desert Shield" toward Operation "Desert Storm."

Above Right: Although modern communications allowed the U.S. commanders and their political leaders to keep in constant touch, some matters were best discussed face-to-face. This photograph shows Secretary Cheney and General Powell with General Schwarzkopf during a visit to Saudi Arabia.

Right: General Schwarzkopf had a mass of military matters to hold his attention right through his long working hours, but he appreciated the importance of press briefings and became a "media star" of the war.

storage bunkers and their launchers, both fixed and mobile. With this task completed, the air forces could finally turn to the destruction of the Iraqi infrastructure and the Iraqi forces in Kuwait. As General Powell said of the Iraqi strength in Kuwait, "First we're going to cut it off, and then we're going to kill it."

The "Scud" Campaign

The air campaign achieved extraordinary success in all aspects but the elimination of the "Scuds." Although storage bunkers and fixed sites were soon destroyed, the Iraqis had moved out many of the missiles, and their truck-based launchers had been carefully disguised as ordinary vehicles for movement to any of the many sites that had been selected and surveyed. Saddam Hussein was astute enough to realize that perhaps his greatest chance of checking the allied campaign was by dividing the coalition, and that his best chance to achieve this end came from provoking anti-Israeli sentiment in the Arab members of the coalition. Having tried and failed to whip up such feeling during the period leading to the beginning of hostilities, the Iraqi leader saw another

Right: At the technical level, the undoubted "weapon star" of the war with Iraq was the Raytheon MIM-104 Patriot surface-to-air missile. This is the traversing and elevating launcher for the weapon, complete with four containerized missiles, of Delta Battery, 11th Air Defense Artillery, normally based at Fort Bliss, Texas.

Below: Men of an explosive ordnance disposal team assigned to the 4409th Combat Support Group, Eastern Liaison Force, recover part of an Iraqi "Scud" missile found 24 miles northwest of Riyadh, the Saudi Arabian capital.

Left: Two MIM-104 Patriot surface-to-air missile launchers are silhouetted against the setting sun in a scene that will remain an enduring reminder of the war against Iraq.

Below: Military personnel examine the spot where the nosecone of a ''Scud'' missile landed before the remains are removed for detailed examination.

chance after the beginning of the war.

Israel had never concealed its national policy of massive retaliation to any and every Arab attack on Israel, and Saddam Hussein now tried to provoke such a reaction with "Scud" missile attacks, hoping that Israeli retaliation on an Arab country might cause Syria, and possibly Saudi Arabia and Egypt, to drop out of the coalition.

Almost exactly 24 hours after the start of the allied air campaign against Iraq, Israeli air-raid sirens began to wail as radar detected incoming missiles. Israel had prepared for such an eventuality in the issue of gas masks, atropine-filled syringes for use on people affected by nerve agents, and an extensive effort to make at least one room in each house at least partially airtight. These sensible precautions were in fact not needed, for despite his threats Saddam Hussein never unleashed "Scuds" carrying chemical warheads. All those used in the war carried only conventional high-explosive charges.

Several missiles were fired in the first wave against Israel, two landing in Tel Aviv and another two in Haifa. By a virtual miracle, direct casualties were a mere 12 injured, but a baby girl died as her parents tried to get her gas mask on, and three elderly women suffocated because they did not take the protective caps off their gas mask filters.

This was just the first in a series of sporadic but sustained attacks against targets in Israel and Saudi Arabia, the last and most devastating taking place on February 25, when the 81st and last missile landed on a temporary barracks in the Saudi Arabian city of Dhahran, killing 28 American servicemen personnel.

Enter the Patriot

The allied air forces made every effort they could to locate and destroy the missiles and their launchers, but the latters' mobility made this a virtually impossible task. Many launchers were indeed found

M1A1 Abrams main battle tanks of the 3rd Armored Division moving from their tactical assembly point in the direction of their forward assembly point for Operation "Desert Storm."

Opposite Top: Men of the 4th Marine Expeditionary Brigade come ashore on the coast of Saudi Arabia from LCUs (Landing Craft Utility) of the amphibious assault ship U.S.S. *Nassau.*

Opposite Below: Men of the 1st Battalion, 2nd Marine Regiment, dig in against a possible counterattack during an amphibious assault operation on the Saudi Arabian coast.

and "killed," but others survived to fire more missiles. The three factors in the allies' favor were the age of the basic missile, which reduced its reliability and accuracy, the poor workmanship of Iraqi modifications, which resulted in many missiles breaking up in flight, and the availability of the Raytheon MIM-104 Patriot surface-to-air missile system.

Although it had been designed as an antiaircraft weapon, the Patriot had recently been upgraded for a limited antimissile capability, and it proved itself one of the wonder weapons of the war. Deployed in Saudi Arabia and Israel, Patriots managed to destroy most of the incoming "Scuds," although not high enough or completely enough to prevent all damage from falling debris. The greatest success claimed by the Patriot came on January 20, when Patriots downed all eight "Scuds" launched at Riyadh and Dhahran.

It was clear from an early stage, therefore, that the allies had a technical edge over the "Scud." Thus the missile was not in itself a major threat. A far more serious threat, however, was the possibility of Israeli retaliation. Perhaps the greatest American diplomatic success of the war lay in persuading the Israeli government not to retaliate, an immensely difficult task that was finally achieved in part by the rapid relocation of American-manned Patriot batteries to Israel.

As the "Scud" campaign continued, the allied air campaign was also pressed with great vigor as its emphasis switched to the Iraqi forces in Kuwait. They were now effectively cut off from Iraq and began to suffer terrible losses of men and materiel in incessant day and night attacks by allied aircraft. Allied intelligence reported that there were now 42 Iraqi divisions in Kuwait with an overall

Crews check out their M1A1 Abrams main battle tanks before Company "A," 1st Cavalry Regiment, moves out for a live-firing exercise during the buildup to Operation "Desert Storm." Although the long buildup of Operation "Desert Shield" had small but nonetheless unfortunate effects on morale, it also allowed personnel to become acclimatized to the region, and their weapons to be thoroughly checked under real operating conditions.

Right: A sand-goggled soldier takes a brief rest during the outflanking envelopment of the Iraqi right flank during Operation "Desert Storm."

Below: Part of the American buildup for Operation "Desert Storm" involved the improvement of operation standards among some of the allied forces. Here men of the 1st Battalion, 325th Airborne Infantry Regiment, demonstrate the technique of overcoming obstacles to Saudi Arabian national guard officers during a live-firing exercise.

strength of between 540,000 and 570,000 troops. What remained unknown, however, was the real effect of the allied air campaign on the manpower and materiel strength of these divisions, and also on their morale and overall fighting efficiency. It became clear only after the end of hostilities that many formations had been under strength from the beginning, that the air campaign had been truly devastating, and that on the eve of the allied land assault, there were "only" 350,000 Iraqi soldiers in Kuwait. The allied planners had to assume the worst possible scenario, however, and therefore tailored their efforts to virtually full-strength opposition.

Erroneous Lesson of the War with Iran

Iraq's experience in the war with Iran had

Opposite: A BGM-109 Tomahawk land-attack cruise missile leaves its Armored Box Launcher Mk 143 on board the nuclear-powered cruiser U.S.S. *Mississippi* in the Red Sea.

Above: A watchful moment of respite for members of the crew of the battleship U.S.S. *Wisconsin* during preparations for the launch of BGM-109 Tomahawk cruise missiles from the ship's patrol station in the Persian Gulf.

been terrible, but it had also been tactically stultifying, as most offensives were undertaken frontally after lengthy preparation. The Iraqi army seems to have assumed that the allies would fight the same way and therefore saw its only chance of victory as checking the allied forces in strong defensive lines where they could not use their superior mobility and could therefore be destroyed by the Iraqi artillery and the combined infantry and armor reserves. Thus the frontier with Saudi Arabia had been fortified with a series of linear defenses such as sand ramparts, barbed wire, minefields, and oil-filled trenches. This defensive line extended to a depth of nearly 19 miles and was held by the notional 350,000 troops of 22 divisions. These infantry formations were arranged two divisions

deep, with one division to every 19 miles of front. Behind this static position was the immediate reserve of 12 divisions, a mobile force divided into three groups deployed from southeast to northwest behind the front-line force with a notional 100,000 men and large numbers of tanks, other armored fighting vehicles, and artillery. Straddling the Kuwaiti border with Iraq was the general reserve: eight Republican Guard divisions with a notional 120,000 men and 1,000 tanks, most of them advanced Soviet-supplied T-72s.

Schwarzkopf knew exactly what the Iraqis expected and planned to do. As he himself put it, "Saddam must have thought we were going to fight him the way the Iranians did. He thought we were going to have one or two days of

One of the 16-inch (406-mm) caliber Mk 7 guns of the U.S.S. *Wisconsin*'s No.3 triple turret unleashes its projectile during a gunnery exercise during Operation "Desert Shield."

preparation and then we were going to come in mass attacks across the ground into his fire trenches, barbed wire, and minefields. His soldiers were going to fall back and they were going to attrit us and attrit us, and about the time we got to the middle of Kuwait and we were severely weakened, he was going to unleash the Republican Guard from the northern border and they were going to come screaming down and counterattack and kill us all."

General Schwarzkopf's Plans

Schwarzkopf was determined not to do as the Iraqis expected. Of the several alternative options available, the two most attractive were an amphibious assault on the Kuwaiti coast near Kuwait City, combined with a land assault north along the coast, or a punch through the comparatively weak western end of the Iraqi defenses with a view to pushing into

central Kuwait to tempt the Iraqis out of their strong defensive positions for destruction by allied air power.

Fairly early in the planning phase, Schwarzkopf decided that the amphibious operation was too obvious a move and opted for the western punch. As the air campaign continued, however, the Iraqis continued to extend their defense line to the west. During October, therefore, Schwarzkopf came to the conclusion that the allies' main effort would not be any sort of frontal assault at all, but rather a huge mobile wheel around the western end of the Iraqi defenses to push sideways into Kuwait behind the frontal defenses in the area where the Iraqis' immediate reserves were located, taking them in the flank.

As the general himself put it, the Iraqi defense was "getting thicker and thicker, and heavier and heavier. But it wasn't going any farther out to the west. So I remembered the fact that in desert war-

fare, you can deceive your enemy as to the point of the main attack. And I said : 'That's it. That's the key.'''

As always, secrecy was the key to success. It was all the more important here, for if the Iraqis had scented what the allies were planning, they could easily have extended their defensive line still farther to the west. Yet keeping the plan secret would be difficult, for it demanded the movement of very large forces over considerable distances of desert even before the offensive began. One of the keys to the allied deception plan was undertaken in the Persian Gulf, where the U.S. Marines' amphibious forces made fairly obvious preparations for a coastal assault, thereby attracting the attention of the Iraqis to the eastern end of the front.

From late October, the definitive plan began to take shape. At their own request, the British and French were given major parts to play, and while it involved the French in no large-scale

Above: This Iraqi tanker was detected and attacked by the allies south of the Khauer al Kakfa oil terminal in the Persian Gulf.

Opposite Top: An M113 armored personnel carrier of the Free Kuwait Forces crosses a trench during a capabilities demonstration.

Opposite Below: Launch of a BGM-109 Tomahawk land-attack cruise missile from an Armored Box Launcher Mk 143 of an American surface warship.

As the Iraqi army in Kuwait disintegrated in the face of the allied land offensive, many men tried to flee into southern Iraq. As those "fortunate" enough to seize motor transport moved north along the few roads of the region, they became easy prey for the allied air forces and suffered enormous losses. Photographed south of Basra, these ravaged vehicles were just some of the many thousands of trucks, buses, and automobiles caught in the open by allied air power and destroyed.

troop movement, the British had to be shifted away from their involvement with the marines without attracting the attention of the Iraqis.

The Final Plan Emerges

In its definitive form, Schwarzkopf's plan called for the XVIII Corps to wheel into the Iraqi west flank and cut the Iraqis' line of retreat, and then for the heavier VII Corps, with the British 1st Armoured Division, to smash the Iraqis' main strength. Just before the XVIII Corps moved off, the Iraqi front was to be pinned by the 2nd Marine Division, while western flank protection was to be provided by the rapid advance of the 82nd Airborne Division supported by the French 6th Armored Division.

The task of moving 3½ divisions from points south of Kuwait to other points 500 miles to the northwest offered considerable logistic problems in its own right and was compounded by the need

The devastation inflicted on the fleeing Iraqi forces by allied aircraft is all the more striking when seen from the ground.

to do so in utmost secrecy. The solution involved the creation of "ghost divisions" to simulate the divisions that were moving and so keep the attention of the Iraqis.

The movement itself involved 150,000 men and large quantities of materiel. It was completed in the last few days before the planned offensive to give the Iraqis as little time as possible to discover the deception and alter their dispositions. Despite the distance to be covered and the limited capacity of the Saudi Arabian road network in this region, the task was accomplished without too much difficulty. As a result, the strength of XVIII Corps doubled from its normal complement of 70,000 men and now operated no fewer than 23,000 vehicles, while the heavier VII Corps had 36,000 vehicles. All was finally ready, and Schwarzkopf had at his disposal 14 divisions (nine American, three Arab, one British, and one French).

By the beginning of February, intelligence reports about the dismal state of the Iraqi forces was being confirmed by

By the time of the allied land offensive, the Iraqi forces in Kuwait had lost a large proportion of their armored strength to allied air attack, and the surviving main battle tanks were further decimated in the allied advance.

On January 11, 1991, the Senate completed a searching debate about the wisdom of going to war. Most Democrats opposed war, including Majority Leader George Mitchell. The "President" he refers to is the honorary head of the Senate:

Mr. President, for two centuries, Americans have debated the relative powers of the President and Congress. Often it has been an abstract argument. But today that debate is real.

The men who wrote the Constitution had as a central purpose the prevention of tyranny in America. They had lived under a British king. They did not want there ever to be an American king. They were brilliantly successful. In our history there have been 41 Presidents and no kings.

The writers of our Constitution succeeded by creating a government with separate institutions and divided powers. They correctly reasoned that if power were sufficiently dispersed, no institution or individual could gain total power.

Nowhere has their concept been more severely tested than in what they regarded as one of the greatest powers of government – the power to make war. . . .

Two days ago, the President requested that Congress authorize him to implement the U.N. resolution authorizing "all necessary means" to expel Iraq from Kuwait.

But yesterday the President said that, in his opinion, he needs no such authorization from the Congress. I believe the correct approach was the one taken by the President two days ago when he requested authorization. His request clearly acknowledged the need for congressional approval.

The Constitution of the United States is not and cannot be subordinated to a U.N. resolution.

So today the Senate undertakes a solemn constitutional responsibility: To decide whether to commit the Nation to War. In this debate, we should focus on the fundamental question before us: What is the wisest course of action for our Nation in the Persian Gulf crisis? . . .

We supported the President's effort in marshaling international diplomatic pressure and the most comprehensive economic embargo in history against Iraq.

I support that policy. I believe it remains the correct policy, even though the President abandoned his own policy before it had time to work.

The change began on November 8, when

President Bush announced that he was doubling the number of American troops in the Persian Gulf to 430,000 in order to attain a "credible offensive option."

The President did not consult with Congress about that decision. He did not try to build support for it among the American people. He just did it.

In so doing, President Bush transformed the U.S. role and its risks in the Persian Gulf crisis.

In effect, the President – overnight, with no consultation and no public debate – changed American policy from being part of a collective effort to enforce economic and diplomatic sanctions into a predominantly American effort relying upon the use of American military force. . . .

I believe the best course now for the President and for the Nation is to "stay the course," to continue the policy the President so clearly established at the outset of the crisis. It offers the best hope now for the achievement of our objectives at the lowest cost in lives and treasure. That is a goal we all share. . . .

And the truly haunting question, which no one will ever be able to answer, will be: Did they die unnecessarily? For if we go to war now, no one will ever know if sanctions would have worked if given a full and fair chance.

Also speaking against the war was the Chairman of the Senate Armed Services Committee, Sam Nunn of Georgia:

In summary, Mr. President, I believe that on balance there is a reasonable expectation that continued economic sanctions, backed up by the threat of military force and international isolation, can bring about Iraq's withdrawal from Kuwait. I believe that the risks associated with the continued emphasis on sanctions are considerably less than the very real risk associated with war and, most importantly, the aftermath of war in a very volatile region of the world.

Mr. President, in conclusion, a message to Saddam Hussein: you are hearing an impassioned debate emanating from the U.S. Capitol, both the House and the Senate. These are the voices of democracy. Do not misread the debate. If war occurs, the constitutional and policy debates will be suspended, and Congress will provide the American troops in the field whatever they need to prevail. There will be no cutoff of funds for our troops while they engage Iraq in battle.

President Bush, the Congress, and the American people are united that you must leave Kuwait. We differ on whether these goals can best be accomplished by administering pain slowly with an economic blockade or by dishing it out in large doses with military power. Either way, Saddam Hussein, you lose. . . .

Mr. President, in closing, I believe that before this Nation is committed to what may be a large-scale war, each of us in the Senate of the United States, in reaching a decision which will be very personal and very difficult for all of us, should ask ourselves a fundamental question: Will I be able to look the parents, the wives, husbands, and children in the eye and say that their loved ones sacrificed their lives for a cause vital to the United States and that there was no other reasonable alternative?

Mr. President, at this time, I cannot.

On January 16, 1991, President Bush announced to the nation that the war had begun:

Just two hours ago, allied air forces began an attack on military targets in Iraq and Kuwait. These attacks continue as I speak. Ground forces are not engaged.

This conflict started August 2nd when the dictator of Iraq invaded a small and helpless neighbor. Kuwait – a member of the Arab League and a member of the United Nations – was crushed; its people brutalized. Five months ago, Saddam Hussein started this cruel war against Kuwait. Tonight, the battle has been joined. . . .

As I report to you, air attacks are underway against military targets in Iraq. We are determined to knock out Saddam Hussein's nuclear bomb potential. We will also destroy his chemical weapons facilities. Much of Saddam's artillery and tanks will be destroyed. Our operations are designed to best protect the lives of all the coalition forces by targeting Saddam's vast military arsenal. Initial reports from General Schwarzkopf are that our operations are proceeding according to plan.

Our objectives are clear. Saddam Hussein's forces will leave Kuwait. The legitimate government of Kuwait will be restored to its rightful place and Kuwait will once again be free.

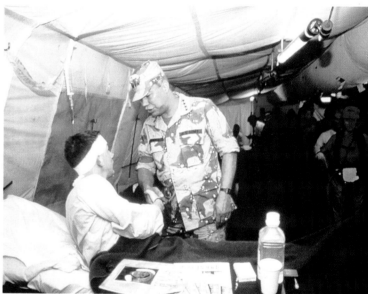

Top: During the buildup of Operation "Desert Shield," the allies practiced the rapid evacuation of casualties in large numbers. Mercifully, however, the actual allied casualty rate was very low.

Below: General Colin Powell talks to a patient at a forward-based medical facility in Saudi Arabia.

One of the worst excesses committed by the Iraqi forces occupying Kuwait was the torching of several hundred oil wells as they fled before the victorious allies. This aerial photograph reveals just part of the grim scene outside Kuwait City.

special force units operating clandestinely behind the Iraqi lines, and Schwarzkopf decided that the time was approaching, but had not yet arrived, for the land campaign to start. Washington was still not sure, however, and on February 9, Cheney and Powell visited Riyadh for a meeting with Schwarzkopf and his command team. The upshot of the meeting was that Cheney and Powell recommended an early start for political and diplomatic reasons, while Schwarzkopf recommended a slight delay to give the air campaign time to inflict still more damage on the disintegrating Iraqi army in Kuwait.

On February 14, it was decided that

the offensive would start seven days later, and two days after that, VII Corps made its move northwest to its new operational area. There were a few last-minute attempts to avoid the land campaign by persuading Saddam Hussein that defeat was inevitable, but even President Gorbachev got nowhere with the intransigent Iraqi leader. President Bush finally decided on February 21 to give Iraq two more days, but Saddam Hussein remained defiant.

The Land War Starts

The land offensive started at 4:00 a.m. on February 24, even though some 2,000

From the journal of an Air Force captain. She served in the Gulf War as an aircraft maintenance fficer, working on 20 F-117A "Stealth" aircraft – one of which was flown in combat by her husband.

October 30, 1990, Saudi Arabia

We've been "in Kingdom" since the 20th of August, so I'll have to go back and try to record our history here to date.

As we prepare to deploy, it appeared we would go to war shortly after our arrival. I was very glad D. and I would be together, but I was worried for him – for 5 hours in an F-117A to Langley AFB, VA, then 14 hours across the pond to Saudi, and of course for possible combat missions to Iraq. I arrived in Saudi Arabia after about 21 hours on a C-5 [military transport].

November 1, 1990

We arrived at this base at about 9 p.m. No one was really expecting us, it seemed. We were the Advan team – 1st to land. There were a couple of Americans who are stationed here and lots of Saudis. They took us out into the dark middle of nowhere to our aircraft shelters – spooky. Saudi patrols driving around in machine gun clad jeeps. Waited all night for cargo that didn't show up until sunrise. I still don't know where I'll sleep. Worked through the next evening then piled on a bus to the housing area. Looks like base housing at any desert base, USA. I get to the women's house and crash on the floor after a shower. During this 24 hour day the aircraft arrived. We had only 2 firemen's ladders and eventually 2 B-1 stands to catch 18 jets. It was a challenge getting the guys out of the cockpit.

The next day I moved back to the shelter area. The room is 2 bunks beds and 4 lockers, one card table size table with one chair. The bath – coed – is down the hall – 2 showers, 2 toilets, 2 urinals, and 3 sinks. We all have to learn to be coed. We all get used to it quickly. D. lives on the other end of the hangar complex with 3 other pilots.

Maintenance is trying to get ready to fly from 3 locations with no vehicles but a couple tugs, and no working radios. We ran out of potable water regularly and became perilously low on MREs [meals ready to eat] during this time. It was

bad. The first chow hall opened and was quite good. After several days of little food and water it was great! Unfortunately, that chow hall only lasted about 5 days until they finalized another contract – Saudi catering – bad. Lots of gristle, bone, and hair in the food.

We went probably 2 weeks without any vehicles – then we got bikes, then trucks. Boy were my feet sore at first.

The other units' arrival has been stressful. Lots of us getting kicked out of our happy homes. I lost my office and my room. People are stealing furniture right and left. It's almost as if you're not sitting on your chair, someone will take it.

January 21, 1991

Christmas was tense. I worked Christmas Eve – we were on alert. There was a terrorist threat for about 0130 Christmas morning, so we were tensed waiting for something to happen. There was a party in a hangar which we attended in shifts because of the terrorist threat.

Since Christmas the peace has been quick. I didn't believe things would really change much – even after 15 Jan., but I was wrong. D. flew his firsr combat sortie 17 Jan. '91. I was worried . . . He's flown twice now. It was easier the second time, but not easy. Stealth technology does work, but antiaircraft artillery doesn't discriminate. A lucky shot is still a lucky shot.

Mail ceased when the war started. We're not getting parts either. I guess the C-130s are dedicated to other stuff.

March 31, 1991

I'm writing on leg two of our journey home. My Aircraft Maintenance Unit flew 1033 combat sorties dropping 677 bombs. We kept up a hectic pace throughout the war, flying 12 × 6* or 12 × 4 (with very short turn time). Toward the end of the war, many said we fought like we were losing because we (for a few nights) attempted to launch the fleet even though the weather was bad. We flew a wing 32 × 32 one night, dropping only 8 bombs. It was crazy.

There was elation, yet disbelief, when the war ended. I didn't trust it but it's holding true.

*[This number means 12 planes flew sorties and returned, and then 6 of them went out a second time.]

On February 27, 1991, President Bush announced military victory:

Kuwait is liberated. Iraq's army is defeated. Our military objectives are met. Kuwait is once more in the hands of Kuwaitis, in control of their own destiny. We share in their joy — a joy tempered only by our compassion for their ordeal.

Tonight the Kuwaiti flag once again flies above the capital of a free and sovereign nation. And the American flag flies above our embassy.

Seven months ago, America and the world drew a line in the sand. We declared that the aggression against Kuwait would not stand. And tonight, America and the world have kept their word.

This is not a time of euphoria; certainly not a time to gloat. But it is a time of pride — pride in our troops; pride in the friends who stood with us in the crisis; pride in our nation and the people whose strength and resolve made victory quick, decisive, and just. And soon we will open wide our arms to welcome back home to America our magnificent fighting forces. . . .

This war is now behind us. Ahead of us is the difficult task of securing a potentially historic peace. Tonight, though, let us be proud of what we have accomplished. Let us give thanks to those who risked their lives. Let us never forget those who gave their lives. May God bless our valiant military forces and their families. And let us all remember them in our prayers.

A technician of Company "D," 1st Battalion, 101st Aviation Brigade, works on the powerplant of a McDonnell Douglas Helicopters AH-64A Apache battlefield helicopter in preparation for a mission from its base in northern Saudi Arabia. The dust and desert sand in the region caused great wear inside engines and other machinery, so good maintenance was essential to guarantee continued flight safety and operational capability.

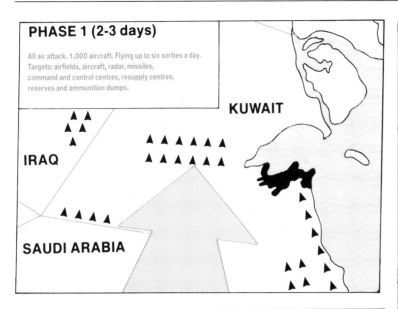

PHASE 1 (2-3 days)

All air attack. 1,000 aircraft. Flying up to six sorties a day. Targets: airfields, aircraft, radar, missiles, command and control centres, resupply centres, reserves and ammunition dumps.

KUWAIT

IRAQ

SAUDI ARABIA

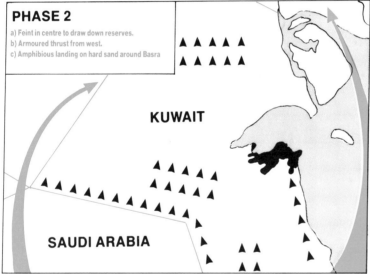

PHASE 2

a) Feint in centre to draw down reserves.
b) Armoured thrust from west.
c) Amphibious landing on hard sand around Basra

KUWAIT

SAUDI ARABIA

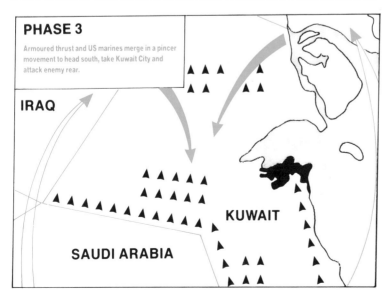

PHASE 3

Armoured thrust and US marines merge in a pincer movement to head south, take Kuwait City and attack enemy rear.

IRAQ

KUWAIT

SAUDI ARABIA

Above: This apparently undamaged main battle tank, a Soviet-supplied T-62, was abandoned by its Iraqi crew on the outskirts of Kuwait City.

Left: This triplet of maps suggests the offensive options that were open to General Norman Schwarzkopf and his planners during Operation "Desert Shield." In the end, the commander of the allied forces opted for the crushing left hook that took Operation "Desert Storm" to complete success in just 100 hours of fast-moving land warfare.

Left: With the sun obscured by smoke from blazing oil wells during the day and the sky illuminated by lurid flames at night, it was often difficult to tell day from night in the days after the Iraqi rout in Kuwait.

This Soviet-built T-55 main battle tank was knocked out as its Iraqi crew tried to escape the allied offensive.

marines had infiltrated through the Iraqi lines two days earlier during a rain storm to prepare the way for a rapid marine advance to Kuwait City.

Taken by complete surprise, the Iraqi forces crumbled from virtually the moment the allies hit them. The course of this fast-moving campaign is best des-

cribed by the accompanying map; w[ith] few exceptions, the allies did exactly they intended. Supplies kept up w[ith] the forward elements, allowing them proceed as planned, and even wh[en] they encountered the first Republic[an] Guard units, the allied forces faced real opposition.

The campaign lasted for exactly 100 hours before a ceasefire ended the misery of the Iraqis. The Iraqis had lost some 3,850 tanks and many tens of thousands of men, whereas allied materiel and personnel losses were small.

Kuwait was free, even though the shattered Iraqis had completed their work of plundering of the country by firing several hundred oil wells as they fled back toward the Iraqi frontier.

A Halt Called Too Soon?

For political reasons, however, it was

127

Right: American forces and equipment to Saudi Arabia in preparation for Operation "Desert Storm." This is an M548 of Battery "B," 318th Field Artillery Battalion, 212th Field Artillery Brigade. Racked outside the vehicle are M16 assault rifles.

Below: Kuwaiti refugees scramble with their meager possessions onto a truck for the return to their homeland.

Allied forces join Kuwaitis in a celebration of the liberation after the surrender of the last Iraqis.

decided to press Iraq no further at the military level. The United Nations has ordered the restoration of all goods and treasures looted in the occupation of Kuwait and ordered Iraq to forfeit one-third of its oil revenues to finance the reconstruction of Kuwait. Yet Saddam Hussein remained in power and turned his malignant attentions to the opposition in his own country. A religious rebellion in the south was put down with great brutality, and a major effort was made against the Kurds in the north. This latter resulted in a huge exodus of Kurdish refugees into Iran and Turkey, and among the international efforts to remedy the situation was the establishment of a secure zone in northern Iraq. Created by the victorious allies in a move from southeastern Turkey, this zone has seen the return of many Kurds trusting in the protection of soldiers of the United States and it allies, though the task of supervising the zone is due to be assumed by the United Nations.

Joyous families await the return of their soldiers after a short
campaign that many had dreaded would be another long and
bloody war for American servicemen.

On March 27, 1991, General Norman Schwarzkopf talked with television reporter David Frost about the recently concluded war. Frost asked the general how he devised his plan:

You make your plan based upon what we call "METTT," mission, enemy, terrain, troops available and time.

And so you made an analysis of all those – and the big factor was really the terrain, the troops available and the enemy – when you looked at the way they were deploying their forces in Kuwait . . . . It was very simple. They had an open flank over there . . . . I said, all right, if he stays in this configuration that he's in right now and if that terrain over on the left flank – his right flank – is, in fact, trafficable, we have a wonderful opportunity to cut off and destroy his forces.

And I've got to tell you, every morning when I would get out of bed, the first thing I would do is go look at the map to see where his forces were and whether or not he was, in fact, extending his forces further out and, more importantly, building these very, very heavy obstacles and barriers in front of his forces, which could have given us a lot of problems.

But, the more you watched his deployment of forces, the more he was stuffing forces into a bag, for all intents and purposes, called Kuwait. And, he was not defending that flank. . . . .

The day we executed the air campaign, I said, "We gotcha." Because . . . then it was impossible . . . for them to reinforce that flank. At that time, we'd still kept all our forces over in the east. They had reacted beautifully to all of our forces being in the east. We had nothing in the west . . . now I knew that, number one, I could move the forces without him being able to see them and, more importantly, even if he saw them, he couldn't do anything about it because we were going to control the air and, had he tried to go out there and do that, we could have gone ahead. So, that's when I knew, "We gotcha."

Frost asked how Schwarzkopf felt about the heavy Iraqi losses:

You have mixed emotions. Your first choice is not to go to war because you know war kills people. So obviously my first choice all along would be, hey, if we could solve this situation, bring peace to the Middle East and not kill a single soldier, that's the best way to resolve this whole thing. If, on the other hand, we have to go to war, then we don't want our hands tied behind our back. We are going to do it 100 percent all the way and do whatever is necessary to inflict maximum casualties on the enemy and minimum on our own forces.

The war was not our choosing. The war was their choosing. They had ample opportunity to avoid the war. . . . I think to be a military commander, you have to have that attitude and that is, "Look, war is not of my choosing, but, when it comes, my objective is to keep as many of my people alive as I can," and you do that by inflicting the maximum casualties on your enemy.

I'm not proud of killing or of being responsible for the death of a single person. I never will be. But, perhaps, by the loss of those lives, we have saved literally hundreds of thousands more in this entire region for many, many years to come and I like to think of it in those terms.

Asked about the war's lessons, the general replied:

There's so many lessons, but I think that there is one really fundamental military truth. And that's that you can add up the correlation of forces. You can look at the number of tanks. You can look at the number of airplanes. You can look at all these factors of military might and put them together, but unless the soldier on the ground or the airman in the air has the will to win – has the strength of character to go into battle, believes that his cause is just and has the support of his country – unless you have that, all the rest is irrelevant.

The difference was, really, when you get right down to it, the fighting spirit of the individual going into combat. And, you see, I am convinced that because of the support of the world that our soldiers, sailors, airmen, and the marines from the entire coalition knew what they had behind them – that gave them a great, great advantage that the Iraqi forces didn't have.

Glossary

Aircraft carrier The type of warship that took over from the battleship as the world's most important type of capital ship during World War II; in essence, a floating airfield with provision for hangering, maintaining and operating a substantial number of aircraft.

Antitank missile A special type of missile generally fired from a ground- or vehicle-based launcher and guided to its target by commands transmitted to the missile over wires unrolled from its rear. The missile flies comparatively slowly, for the hollow-charge warhead carried by such missiles works best at a low impact speed.

Armored personnel carrier A vehicle designed to move troops on the battlefield; generally a tracked vehicle that protects the troops inside against small arms fire. Personnel are generally carried in a compartment at the rear of the vehicle with access, in the case of the American M113, through a powered rear ramp/door.

Artillery An overall term for tube weapons that fire shells instead of bullets, and which are too large and complex for one person to operate alone.

Ballistic missile A missile which does not rely on aerodynamic surfaces for lift. It therefore follows a "ballistic," or thrown, trajectory after the end of its engine burn.

Battalion A basic subdivision of the regiment, generally made up of less than 1,000 men and commanded by a lieutenant colonel.

Blockade A naval and/or air campaign to deny the enemy or neutrals access to or departure from the enemy's ports and coast.

Bomber An airplane designed to deliver free-fall bombs, therefore a comparatively large type with greater range than the fighter; generally carries its offensive weapons in a lower-fusalage bomb bay and has gun turrets for defense against enemy fighters.

Brigade A basic subdivision of a division, generally including two or more battalions and commanded by a brigadier general (see *Regiment*).

Company The basic subdivision of a battalion, generally less than 200 men and commanded by a captain.

Corps A primary component of the army, made up of two or more divisions and commanded in the U.S. Army by a major general, but in most other armies by a lieutenant general.

Cruise missile A type of subsonic missile that flies to its target using aerodymanic lift rather than ballistic flight.

Cruiser A warship next up in size from the destroyer and generally equipped with the sensors and weapons to undertake the antiaircraft, antiship, and antisubmarine roles, although the capabilities in one or two of these tasks are generally higher than in the third.

Destroyer A warship intermediate in size and capability between a frigate and a cruiser. One of any navy's "workhorse" vessels, it combines affordability with high performance and is the right size to be fitted with a useful sensor and appropriate weapons.

Division The smallest army formation, containing two or more brigades and commanded by a major general. It is the basic organization designed for independent operation and therefore contains support elements (artillery, engineers, etc.) in addition to its infantry.

Flank The extreme right or left of a body of troops in a military position.

Formation Any large body of troops organized with the capability for operations independent of the rest of the army and therefore possessing, in addition to its organic infantry units, a full range of artillery, engineer, and support services. The smallest formation is generally the division.

Frigate A warship next down in size from the destroyer. It is generally fitted for a single, specific role, with a subsidiary for a second task capability.

Gun One of the basic weapons of the artillery; a high-velocity weapon with a comparatively long barrel designed for direct engagement (firing at an elevation angle below 45°) of targets that can be seen through the weapon's sight.

Howitzer One of the basic weapons of the artillery; a lower-velocity weapon than the gun. It has a comparatively short barrel and is designed for the indirect engagement (firing at an elevation angle of more than 45°) of targets hidden from direct sight by an intervening feature.

Intercontinental ballistic missile (ICBM) A strategic weapon carrying a nuclear warhead or warheads over a range greater than 3,425 miles (5,510 km).'

Interdictor A type of warplane with a range to fly deep into the enemy's rear areas with the mission of destroying lines of communications, supply dumps, reinforcements, and comparable targets.

Logistics The science of planning and carrying out the movement of military forces and their supplies.

Materiel The overall term for equipment, stores, supplies, and spares.

Mine An explosive device generally encased in metal or plastic and designed to destroy or incapacitate vehicles, or to kill or wound personnel. The two basic types of mine are the land mine, a comparatively small weapon which is generally buried in the ground, and the sea mine, a considerably larger weapon either laid on the bottom of shallow waters or, in deeper waters, floating just below the surface at the top of an anchored cable.

Regiment The basic tactical unit subordinate to the division (in the British forces, the brigade) containing two or more battalions and generally commanded by a colonel.

Strategy The art of winning a campaign or war by major operations.

Submarine-launched ballistic missile A strategic missile carrying one or more nuclear warheads and designed to be launched from a submerged and therefore basically undetectable submarine operating underwater anywhere within range of the target.

Surface-to-air missile A specialized missile launched from a ground launcher against aircraft. It uses either its own guidance package or commands transmitted from the ground to home in accurately on the target.

Tanker/transport Transport plane able to undertake both the conventional transport and inflight refueling roles.

Unit Any small body of troops not organized to operate independent of the rest of the army. It therefore does not possess, in addition to its organic infantry units, a full range of artillery, engineer, and support services. The largest unit is the regimental combat team, known in most other armies as the brigade.

Bibliography

Ajami, Fouad. *The Arab Predicament.* (Cambridge University Press, 1981).

Chadwick, Frank. *Desert Shield Fact Book.* (Berkley Books, 1991). A guide to equipment, troops, and tactics.

Congressional Record. (U.S. Government Printing Office, January 10-12, 1991). The Senate Armed Services Committee public hearings.

Dawood, N. J. (translator). *The Koran.* (Viking Penguin, 1990). The holy writings accepted by the world's Muslims as the word of God.

Esposito, John L. *Islam: The Strange Path.* (Oxford University Press, 1990). A comprehensive introduction to Islam, the world's second largest religion.

Fromkin, David. *A Peace to End All Peace: Creating the Modern Middle East 1914-1922.* (Henry Holt and Co., 1989). The struggles in the Middle East in light of the divisions imposed on the region by the Allies after World War One.

Gowers, Andrew and Tony Walker. *Behind the Myth: Yasser Arafat and the Palestinian Revolution.* (W. H. Allen, 1990). A well-told story of the rise from insignificant politician to one of the most newsworthy men alive.

Hiro, Dilip. *The Longest War.* (Routledge, 1991).

al-Khalil, Samir. *Republic of Fear: The Inside Story of Saddam's Iraq.* (Pantheon, 1990). How Saddam Hussein took over Iraq.

Lamb, David. *The Arabs: Journeys Beyond the Mirage.* (Random House, 1987). The issues that confront the Middle East today including the spread of religious extremism, the politics of oil, Israel, and Arab terrorism.

McKinnon, Dan. *Bullseye Iraq.* (Berkley Books, 1990).

Miller, Judith and Mylroie, Laurie. *Saddam Hussein and the Crisis in the Gulf.* (Times Books, 1990). A brisk account of the events leading up to Saddam's invasion of Kuwait.

Sasson, Jean. *The Rape of Kuwait.* (Knightsbridge Publishing, 1991). An uneven account, .its strength being interviews with Kuwaitis.

Sciolino, Elaine. *A Line in the Sand.* (John Wiley & Sons, 1991).

Wilson, George. *Mud Soldiers.* (Charles Scribner's Sons, 1989). A good description of life in the all-volunteer army, providing great insight into the men who fought the war in the Gulf.

Woodward, Bob. *The Commanders.* (Simon & Schuster, 1991). Military decision, making during the first two years of the Bush administration, with special emphasis on the Gulf War.

Yergin, Daniel. *The Prize: The Epic Quest for Oil, Money, and Power.* (Simon & Schuster, 1991).

Index

Page numbers in *Italics* refer
to illustration